PREHISTORIC
LONDON

PREHISTORIC LONDON

THE CAPITAL BEFORE THE ROMANS

SIMON WEBB

PEN & SWORD HISTORY

AN IMPRINT OF PEN & SWORD BOOKS LTD.
YORKSHIRE – PHILADELPHIA

First published in Great Britain in 2025 by
Pen & Sword History
An imprint of
Pen & Sword Books Ltd
Yorkshire - Philadelphia

ISBN 978 1 03610 398 9

Typeset in INDIA by IMPEC eSolutions
Printed and bound in England by CPI Group (UK) Ltd, Croydon, CR0 4YY

The Publisher's authorised representative in the EU for product safety is
Authorised Rep Compliance Ltd., Ground Floor, 71 Lower Baggot Street,
Dublin D02 P593, Ireland.
www.arccompliance.com

For a complete list of Pen & Sword titles please contact:

PEN & SWORD BOOKS LIMITED
George House, Units 12 & 13, Beevor Street,
Off Pontefract Road, Barnsley, S71 1HN, UK
E-mail: enquiries@pen-and-sword.co.uk
Website: www.pen-and-sword.co.uk

or

PEN AND SWORD BOOKS
1950 Lawrence Rd, Havertown, PA 19083, USA
E-mail: uspen-and-sword@casematepublishers.com
Website: www.penandswordbooks.com

Contents

List of Plates

1. The Neolithic burial mound which stands on the edge of an escarpment in Richmond Park.
2. A so-called 'round barrow', a Bronze Age mound on Plumstead Common in south London.
3. A nodule of flint forming the fossil of a sea urchin, found in south London.
4. The ancient seabed of south London.
5. The fossilized remains of sea creatures which lived near London, 55 million years ago.
6. A Palaeolithic hand axe.
7. A sign forbidding people to cast money into a coffin.
8. Rivers of central London, which now flow underground.
9. Prehistoric Southwark, a district of islands.
10. A Neolithic track through a dangerous bog near London.
11. A barrow field near London's Docklands.
12. The so-called 'Waterloo Helmet', over 2,000 years old.
13. A magnificent bronze shield, recovered from the Thames.
14. The Bell Barrow at Hampstead, in central London.
15. The Shrewsbury tumulus.
16. The temple in Greenwich Park.
17. The Dagenham Idol.
18. The way up to the hill fort of Charlton Camp.
19. The view across London from the vicinity of Loughton Camp.
20. Amesbury Banks, where Boudicca's last stand reputedly took place.

Introduction

This book is about prehistoric London; that is to say, London before written records exist. Since the city in this part of the Thames Valley was founded at about the same time that literacy arrived in the British Isles, as a consequence of the Roman invasion in 43 AD, it follows that we shall be trying to piece together the story of what happened around that stretch of the River Thames in the years before this event. There may have been no city where London now stands, before the Romans began building there, but there were certainly people living, working, farming and conducting religious ceremonies in the area. Since they did not write about their lives though, we are forced to sift through the evidence to try and build up a picture of what was happening before the Romans built their city.

The lack of reliable information about London before the coming of the Romans has, in the past, led to wild and fanciful speculations about the early history of this section of the Thames Valley. All we can say with assurance is that the name of the river and also that given to the location where the Roman city became established, both predate the coming of the Romans.

The first mention of the Thames is to be found in Julius Caesar's *Gallic Wars*, in one part of which he describes how he landed forces in Britain and then marched inland, until he came to a river called the Tamesis, which was of course the Thames.

Clearly, it had roughly the same name when Caesar arrived at its banks during the course of his second expedition to Britain, in 54 AD, as it does now. There has been much speculation as to how the Thames came to acquire its name. It has been suggested that it is formed of a combination of two Celtic words; *tam*, meaning wide, and *uisghe*, meaning water. Others believe that the name of the river derives from a Celtic word for 'dark'. The Irish word for dark is *teimheal*, and is from the same root. From this reading, the original name of the Thames might perhaps have meant dark water or black water.

The 'th' with which we now spell the name of the river, has never been pronounced. It was added in the sixteenth century with a view to giving a more classical flavour to London's river. It was thought that the spelling of 'Thames', rather than 'Tames', might make it look vaguely Greek.

In much the same way, we have good reason to suppose that when the Romans called the new settlement Londinium, they were not creating the name from scratch, but rather Latinising an existing place name. It is almost certain that the area in which the city of London now stands was known by a similar name thousands of years ago, but what the derivation of this name might be or what it originally meant is quite beyond our ability to say. Various suggestions have been made, but since none can now be confirmed, such speculations are sterile. What is certain is that whatever was here before the Romans, it was not a large settlement, let alone a city. As far as the evidence is concerned, there is no reason to suppose that there was even a hamlet or village where the invaders founded their city.

The reality of London's origin, that Britain's capital city was founded by invading foreigners who enslaved us, has never been an especially appetizing one to many people and in the medieval period, as this country grew more and more important in European affairs, it was even less palatable. Few people wished to think that British history started with the Roman invasion and that until that time, London had been nothing but a marshy area on the banks of the Thames, with perhaps one or two scattered farmsteads. So it was that a mythical history was devised to fill in the blank page of this part of Britain before 43 AD. The chief architect of this fictious account of early London was a Welsh clergyman known as Geoffrey of Monmouth, who, in a book published in 1135, gave Britain a noble history and set out to show that London had been a glorious city over a thousand years before the Romans ever set foot in the country. Nothing could be more calculated to appeal to the pride of a nation fast becoming an important player on the world stage.

Taking as his pattern the Roman poet Virgil's *Aeneid*, Geoffrey of Monmouth set out a similar plan of early British history. In the *Aeneid*, Virgil told the story of a Trojan hero called Aeneas, who, after the fall of Troy, fled across the Mediterranean and founded the city of Rome. This served to give the Romans a sense that their own civilization and culture was an ancient one and of noble lineage. In his book, *Historia Regum Brittaniae*, Geoffrey of Monmouth uses a similar idea, by claiming that the grandson of Acneas, called Brutus, had himself set off in search of a new land. The goddess Diana spoke to him in a dream, saying,

Brutus, beyond the setting of the sun, past the realms of Gaul there lies an island in the sea, once occupied by giants. Now it is empty and ready for your folk. Down the years this will prove an abode suited to you and your people: and for your descendants it will be a second Troy. A race of kings will be born there from your stock and the round circle of the whole earth will be subject to them.

Little wonder that this captured the imagination of the British people who read it, as it gave them a special place among the nations and showed that they were destined to rule the world!

Although there was not a word of truth in any of this and it had, for the most part, been dreamed up in the fertile imagination of an obscure priest, this legendary origin of Britain, and also London, was accepted as being based on fact for many centuries. It was too enticing a vision to cast away. Britain was, it seemed, named after Brutus and it was he who had founded London, in about 1100 BC. When Brutus decided he needed a capital city, Geoffrey of Monmouth explained how he went about choosing the right location,

He visited every part of the land in search of a suitable spot. He came at length to the River Thames, walked up and down its banks and so chose a site suited to his purpose. There he built his city and called it New Troy.

This is a most attractive story, and it is a pity that it is no more than a fairy tale. It is not hard to see why the made-up story would be seen as preferable to the unattractive truth.

The actual history London before the Roman invasion only emerged over the last couple of centuries or so, in dribs and drabs. There has been no startling and dramatic discovery, like the finding of the city of Pompeii beneath its layer of lava. Rather, the truth came to light gradually, an as an accumulation of small discoveries, each of them slight in themselves, but which slowly allowed an accurate narrative to be constructed of the capital's past. It is largely through the traces of their superstitious beliefs and religion that we have been able to piece together a good deal about the lives of those living thereabouts in the centuries and millennia before the Roman conquest.

The majority of prehistoric artifacts which we have recovered in what is now Greater London were either buried with the dead, or sacrificed to the earth and water in what are known as 'votive offerings'. These are objects which were given to the gods by being buried in the ground or cast into bodies of water, from where they would perhaps be expected to make their way to the underworld. It is from these sources that all the best items of arms and armour, as well as many other things, have been discovered. Because the dead were often provided for in the afterworld, all kinds of goods and belongings were interred with them, and this too has provided valuable evidence of the day-to-day life of people in this area during the Neolithic and Bronze Ages. Nor is this the only way in which burial practices and religious beliefs can help us to build a picture of London before London. It is for this reason that a good deal of this book will be concerned with religion, because it is this which has allowed us to build up a picture of life in the place which would one day become London. One example of how the method of burial has shed light upon the way of life of the living at different times will perhaps be helpful, to illustrate this point.

Very little evidence remains to be seen of the people who lived near this part of the Thames before the Roman invasion. Their homes were built of wood, thatch, moss and mud, and have long since rotted away. However, what do remain in a few places are faint traces of ritual monuments and a few burial mounds, known as barrows. The earliest of these dates from the Neolithic, the time when farmers arrived in Britain from Anatolia and the Middle East, bringing with them a new way of life. As well as the idea of planting wheat and keeping flocks of sheep and herds of goats, these newcomers also had a tradition of erecting what are known as long barrows. These are rectangular mounds, constructed of earth, chalk and stone, where their dead were interred. Centuries later, a new wave of immigrants came, and their ideas for barrows were quite different. They built round mounds for their dead. Just glancing at these different kinds of mound tells us something interesting about the communities who settled in the Thames Valley.

Illustration 1 shows a so-called 'long barrow' in west London's Richmond Park. It is not an impressive prehistoric remain, as Historic England's description in its listing as a Scheduled Monument makes clear,

The mound takes the form of an irregular oval earthwork. The mound is aligned roughly north-south along the scarp-edge, with the land to the west falling away to the Thames, which is approximately one mile away. The mound is approximately 45.0m long, 22.5m wide and up to 3.5m high.

It is in fact a singularly uninspiring muddy hillock, which would be easy to miss, unless you were actually in search of it. Nevertheless, it is of enormous significance, partly because it is the only long barrow which may be seen in Greater London.

Looking now at Illustration 2, we see the type of burial mound which superseded long barrows. This is a round barrow in South London, a saucer-shaped bump on the ground. The interesting point about these different kinds of burial mound is that archaeological excavation in Europe reveals that Neolithic houses were rectangular, while those from the Bronze Age were, by and large, round. This mirrors the original shape of each culture's burial mounds. Time has blurred and eroded the outline of many of the surviving long barrows, such as the one in Richmond Park, but they originally imitated the ground plans of ordinary homes. It has been suggested that this was no coincidence and that the barrows were designed to be, quite literally, houses of the dead. This then may be a case of an archaeological remain relating to religious belief and customs relating to the interment of the dead, which sheds light on the way of life of those who constructed the mounds.

In some parts of the British Isles, the monuments and tombs from the Neolithic were made of stone, but in London, they were constructed from earth. To understand the way of life, and death, in prehistoric London, we need to consider the geology of the area. Cities, especially old cities like London, are usually shaped by geology. Their original position was dictated by the presence or absence of rivers, coasts, mountains and swamps. In the same way, the physical nature of the buildings in a city is frequently connected with what is found nearby, in the way of reefs of rock or layers of clay. If there is a good supply of marble, then this will be used as a building material. If, as is the case with the London area, there is only mud, chalk and clay, then it is those substances from which walls will be made. For this reason, we must begin our story of prehistoric London by examining the geological formations which lie beneath the modern city.

Chapter 1

The Geology of London

Most Londoners are vaguely aware that they live at the bottom of a shallow, bowl-shaped depression in South East England. They know that the land rises to the south and north of the capital, so that High Barnet, in the northern suburbs is indeed high, at least when compared with Westminster, while Crystal Palace is situated on hilly ground on the other side of the river, to the south. That the Chiltern Hills lie to the north and west, while south of the city are the Surrey Hills and the Downs, also makes up part of the Londoner's mental geography. It seldom occurs to anybody in London though, to ask *why* this should be the case. Such things are simply taken for granted and accepted as brute facts, just as is the knowledge that a river runs through their city and flows east to the sea.

The physical structure of the land, together with geographical features such as rivers, hills or proximity to the sea, are what determines the nature and location of a city. Whether a town will grow to be a mighty port or centre of coalmining and industry is inextricably linked to the topography and geology of the area in which it has been built. The presence of a navigable river, seams of easily accessible coal or the presence of certain types of rock, shapes both the purpose and physical structure of cities. The Scottish city of Aberdeen, to give an obvious example, would scarcely have acquired its nickname of the Granite City, were it not for the vast quantities of granite in that part of Scotland, from which so many buildings in Aberdeen have been constructed over the years.

To understand the origins of London, we must first know about the land on which it stands; both the underlying rocks, and the physical features into which they have been carved by flowing water or eroded by wind and rain. Today, London seems inseparable from the River Thames which lies at its heart, but there was a time when the Thames did not even pass through that part of Britain. Were it not for the river, then it is unlikely that Britain's capital city would have been in that part of the country where we find it today. Most European capitals lie on rivers. Budapest and Vienna are on the Danube, Paris is on the Seine, and so on. London is inextricably linked to the river which divides it in two. It was not always so.

In the London Borough of Redbridge is a small and isolated fragment of ancient woodland, called Knighton Wood. This lies on the very edge of the northern border of Greater London. The little patch of forest, entirely surrounded by residential streets, is 10 miles north of the Thames, and it contains a man-made lake which, when constructed, revealed the gravel which lies beneath the ground there. This gravel can still be seen by anybody minded to visit Knighton Wood and examine the shore of the lake. These deposits, which were laid down perhaps half a million years ago by a river which flowed north towards Essex, are known as Woodford Gravel and they are very distinctive. Analysis of the sand and stones indicates that they had their origins in the Weald; that high ridge of land which stretches across Hampshire, Surrey and Kent. For those familiar with a map of London and the surrounding areas, this is very puzzling. How on earth could a river have its origin in Surrey and then flow north to deposit sediments on the border of Essex? Surely, such a watercourse would find its way blocked by the Thames? As it happens, the Thames was not in what we might regard as its usual place at that time. It is a relative newcomer to the district which we now know as the Thames Valley; of which, more later.

Before we look at the River Thames, we must first ask ourselves what London is actually made of; what are the rocks which make up the foundation the city? Unless we know this, then understanding the development of the area where our capital city would one day be founded will prove impossible. It is something which few of those living in London ever trouble to ask themselves. What lies beneath their feet?

There are three main types of rock in the world. These are igneous, sedimentary and metamorphic. Igneous rocks are formed of cooled and solidified magma, the molten rock which lies beneath the earth's crust and sometimes wells up through volcanoes. In the beginning, the earth was a mass of molten rock, which cooled into igneous rocks. These were, for many millions of years, the only kind of rocks to be found anywhere in the world. The granite upon which the city of Aberdeen is built is a typical igneous rock. In London, the igneous rocks lie hundreds of feet below the surface and are never seen. When igneous rock is eroded, by the action of weather or running water, it is broken into tiny grains. These can be swept into the sea by rivers and deposited on the seafloor as a sediment, or sometimes blown by the wind until they built up a deposit on land, known as loess. Over a vast length of time, typically millions of years, these grains, whether under water or on land, can build up to form a new type of rock, which is known as sedimentary. Sometimes sedimentary rock can also be formed from the shells of plankton in the ocean which similarly fall to the seabed and build up into great drifts which solidify over the course of the ages. In this way, rocks like limestone, sandstone and chalk are formed. If, by the movement of tectonic plates, they subsequently end up deep enough under the earth, then the heat and pressure can act upon them and transform them greatly. This process turns limestone into marble, for example. Rocks like that are known as metamorphic. Our brief diversion into geology was necessary so that the landscape of London can fully be appreciated and understood.

It is today fashionable to pretend that ice caps are an essential feature of our planet and that if they were to melt, then all manner of disasters would befall us. This is part of the narrative of climate change which, in the modern world, is always tacitly understood to be something brought about or caused by human activity, chiefly in the form of burning fossil fuels or running factories. In reality, climate change has been with us since there first *was* a climate. Ice caps come and go. A hundred million years ago, Antarctica was a sub-tropical rainforest, teeming with dinosaurs. Today, of course, it is a barren and inhospitable wilderness; the coldest place on earth. At the time that it was covered with vegetation and animal life, much of Britain lay beneath a warm ocean. This was the Cretaceous Era, named from the Latin word for chalk, *'creta'*. It was during this time, from roughly 145 to 66 million years ago, that the chalk which lays beneath South East England, including of course London, was formed.

For tens of millions of years, countless microscopic plankton with shells and plates made of calcium carbonate lived and died in the seas above what would one day become South East England. These organisms are still with us today and they are called foraminifera and coccolithophores. Foraminifera are like tiny snails, less than a millimetre long. Coccolithophores, on the other hand, are neither animals, plants nor fungi. They belong in a class of their own called Protista. Like plants, they use the sun's light to carry out photosynthesis, but unlike plants they also make plates of calcium carbonate, just as many molluscs do. Although it would take a powerful microscope to see a single one of the plates produced in this way, there was a vast number of them during the Cretaceous and, as the little coccolithophores died, their plates fell to the seabed, together with the shells of dead foraminifera. In time, a layer of ooze gradually built up; a soft sludge consisting of many billions of the tiny shells and plates from the plankton. It was a slow process, but on such an enormous timescale, measured not in millions, but tens of millions of years, an immensely thick sediment slowly accumulated. Anybody visiting the White Cliffs of Dover or Beachy Head in Sussex, will see at a glance just how vast were the quantities involved, because those cliffs are made of chalk. This is nothing more than the solidified remains of those billions of tiny fragments of calcium carbonate; each too small to be seen with the naked eye.

It is curious to note that even today, we have no idea why coccolithophores produce these plates, although several theories have been advanced. They are still doing so, but their function remains a mystery. Every time you see a piece of chalk or visit the seaside and sit on the beach beneath a white cliff, you are in the presence of a scientific enigma. This is associated with another slight mystery, one connected with both chalk and the origins of human civilization. This is the precise mechanism behind the formation of flint. Flint is a sedimentary rock, a form of silica, or silicon dioxide, which is harder than iron. It takes the form of nodules which are embedded in chalk and was for well over a million years the substance used by humans to accomplish and carry out almost every conceivable activity; from chopping down trees to killing and butchering animals. It is the 'stone' to which we refer when we talk vaguely of the 'Stone Age'. Flint is a very hard form of silica, similar in many ways to the volcanic rock obsidian. This is a glassy, black material which, like flint, can be shaped into arrowheads, knives and axes. Similar as they may appear in form and function, both are composed chiefly of silicon dioxide; obsidian is an igneous rock, while flint is sedimentary.

Illustration 3 shows a nodule of flint found in south London, not far from Greenwich. It was at one time surrounded by chalk. It will be seen that this piece of flint is actually the fossilized remains of a sea urchin. For centuries, farm workers referred to such things as fairy loaves when they turned up during ploughing. They do bear a slight resemblance to certain types of loaf. When this sea urchin died, it sank into the mud on the seabed, made up of all those pieces of calcium carbonate from dead plankton, and there, over the course of many years, it underwent a miraculous transformation. We all know what a fragile thing is the shell or test of a sea urchin. The way in which such a delicate item has been turned into something harder than iron is a fascinating one. Once the sea urchin rotted away, it left a hollow space within the chalk, a perfect mould of itself. In time, seawater in which was dissolved silicon dioxide from things like sea sponges seeped into the mould and, in a way not fully understood, crystallized out into flint.

The geological structure of this part of the Thames Valley, which led to chunks of flint being scattered across what would one day become London, has been of great significance in the early history of the area, once humans arrived. The earliest people found, laying around, the raw material from which weapons and tools could be fashioned and it was this which resulted in some of the earliest human remains being found at Swanscombe, just outside the border of Greater London. We shall be looking in greater detail at this subject in the next chapter.

For tens of millions of years, the warm sea which covered what would one day become South East England, including of course London, was teeming with plankton, which lived and died until the seabed was covered with their remains. Today, this forms a layer of chalk over 200 yards thick which lies beneath London. In other words, the chalk beneath London is as thick as London's BT Tower is tall. This layer of chalk rises into high land and hills to the north and south of the capital. In some places in London itself, it breaks through and is visible, which leads to some surprising and unexpected sights.

Some people claim that the best views of central London are to be had from the upper floors of the Shard in Southwark. Others favour the London Eye and find the panorama from the top of this famous tourist attraction to be more impressive than that from any office block. As a matter of fact, the partisans of both the Shard and the Eye are equally mistaken. The most extensive and spectacular prospect of inner London costs nothing at all to visit and may be seen from a place of which not one Londoner in a thousand has ever heard. It is a high, chalk promontory overlooking the Thames; a tongue of land jutting out from Blackheath and lying only a few hundred yards from Greenwich Observatory.

Standing on the edge of a cliff is no common experience in London, which serves to make a visit to the patch of ground known as the Point vaguely disconcerting. A grassy area like a miniature park, only a couple of acres or so in area, it is surrounded by railings, which prevent anybody from tumbling down to the back gardens of the houses below. From here, unobstructed by ceilings, floors, window-frames or walls, the view out across London is unrivalled; a 360-degree vista, encompassing not only all the familiar landmarks such as Big Ben and St Paul's Cathedral, but also glimpses of the countryside of Essex.

Beneath this grassy area is a system of chambers, known as Jack Cade's Caverns, which are the remains of a chalk mine. This part of London is riddled with such old mine workings, because digging up chalk and then burning it to make lime has been something carried out in London for thousands of years. The mining extended east from Greenwich all the way to Woolwich and Plumstead. A few years ago, two newly built houses in Plumstead collapsed, due to their having been built above a disused chalk mine. These chalky areas of London are though limited, because the chalk in London is usually overlayed with a heavy mantle of clay. It is this clay which is far more often seen in London and wherever you dig down deep enough, you are sure to encounter it.

Clay is another sedimentary rock. When rivers erode rocks and carry pebbles and sand to the sea, microscopic particles of rocks are also carried out into the ocean. Those minute pieces of grit, less than 0.002mm in size, can settle on the ocean floor. Just as with the formation of chalk, over millions of years, they accumulate on the seabed and eventually form the slippery substance which we know as clay. It is this which has provided the primary building material of the capital. Clay, in various forms, can be turned into bricks. If Aberdeen is the Granite City, then London may not inaptly be called the City of Brick, for it has always been of brick that most of the buildings in London are constructed. The typical yellow 'London Stock' brick is made of London clay. That is all that bricks are really made of, just clay that has been baked hard in kilns. Some are made too from wind-blow deposits of dried dust and silt, which is known as loess. Seams of this material, formed during the Ice Age, were dug up in the nineteenth century and are called 'brickearth'. Clay makes for heavy soils, as any gardener in London will know, but it has the virtue of both retaining water and also being fertile, far more so than sandy or chalky soils.

We might stop for a moment here and consider a point which may not be immediately obvious and that is the role of geology in shaping the history of British cities. Of course, we know that Manchester, as well as some cities in Yorkshire and the English Midlands, were, until a few years ago, the industrial heartlands of this country. It seldom occurs to us though to ask *why* that is the case. Why Birmingham and not Truro? Why Bradford and not the Hampshire city of Winchester? The answer lies in the geology of England.

The Industrial Revolution began with steam engines and then saw the increasingly widespread use of iron and steel. Both these things need coal and so it was logical for factories and steel mills to be sited where the coal was, thus obviating the need to transport this vital raw material over long distances. In the eighteenth century, cities such as Birmingham and Manchester were no more than collections of villages, but since they lie on areas with a good deal of coal to be found beneath them, it was only natural that it was here that industrialization should begin. British history during the nineteenth and twentieth centuries was heavily bound up with the mining and use of coal, which shaped the cities and determined which areas would see factories and mills, and which would remain agricultural backwaters.

When the Bronze Age began in Britain, around 2300 BC, it was inevitable that the centre of the new cultures would be established fairly near to the raw materials necessary for the manufacture of the metal now being used for weapons and tools. Bronze is an alloy or mixture of copper and tin, neither of which are to be found anywhere near London. Tin is however found in Cornwall and copper in Wales, so the centre of British culture was in an area closer to these places than London. This was the Wessex Culture, which flourished in Dorset, Wilshire, Hampshire and Berkshire. The Iron Age though, was a different matter entirely and once again, which parts of the country would become important was dictated largely by geology. In this case it was the southern part of London and the high ground of Surrey and Sussex which would prove to be of great significance.

One of the earliest sites found in Britain where the smelting of iron took place is in London. The reason for this is very simple. Rocks containing a carbonate of iron are found very near to the surface in south London and the hilly district to the south of the capital known as the Weald. This meant that the extraction of iron and the forging of iron objects could take place there, rather than needing to involve any trade routes in distant parts of Britain. Combined with the fact that the River Thames discharged into the North Sea almost exactly opposite the Rhine, which flowed through central Europe, making is easy enough to sail straight from central Europe to the heart of Britain, and it was clear why this part of the Thames Valley became a key location for industry and trade.

In addition to chalk and clay, there is also a good deal of sand, as well as a lot of pebbles under the streets of London. Much of the material which overlays the chalk was laid down something like 55 million years ago, during the period known as the Eocene. It was a time when what is now South East England was still below a shallow, tropical sea. Incredibly, it is actually possible to visit the seabed of this ancient ocean today. It may be found just a short distance from Belmarsh Prison in south London.

Illustration 4 shows the dappled sunlight which plays on the sand which lay below water 55 million years ago. Parts of what is now Britain were underwater at that time, but other bits were not, and the estuaries of various rivers discharged into the sea not far from here. To find this extraordinary place, it is only necessary to take a train on that most modern part of London's transport system, the Elizabeth Line, getting off at Abbey Wood. The abbey in the name of this station refers to Lesnes Abbey, a ruined priory in south London, not far from Woolwich. It is in the nearby woods that we are able to study at first hand the ancient history of London.

A path in Lesnes Abbey Woods leads to a large area of fine sand, such as you might find on a beach. This is the seabed dating back 50 million years or so and a very strange feeling it is, to run this sand through one's fingers. Even more disconcerting is to dig in the sand, for in doing so the detritus of that long-vanished ocean may be unearthed. Illustration 5 shows what may be found in the sand in the course of an hour or so's digging. Here are small seashells, which died tens of millions of years ago, and here too are the teeth of sharks which were swimming above this area at that time. There is something decidedly eerie about poking around in this way on the sea-bottom near the centre of London!

Of course, the land and the sea have changed radically since the time that crocodiles and sharks were to be found navigating the estuaries and weaving through the ocean currents where one of the world's greatest cities would one day stand. This is a consequence partly of the movement of tectonic plates and also of the Ice Age which gripped the planet two million years ago.

As most people know, the continents are not anchored firmly in place on the surface of the earth, but rather sit on vast plates which drift very slowly around on the liquid interior, crashing into each other, splitting in two and occasionally vanishing altogether. It is for this reason that the east coast of South America looks as though it would fit as neatly into the west coast of Africa as the matching pieces of a jigsaw puzzle. At one time, the two continents were part of the same, gigantic landmass which has been named Pangaea. South America split off and began moving west, creating the Atlantic Ocean in the process. The gap between the two continents continues to increase by a distance of roughly an inch each year; that is to say rather more slowly than the speed at which your fingernails are growing. Africa and South America are moving apart, but

40 million years ago, Europe suffered a slow-motion cataclysm as the tectonic plate on which the continent of Africa is found drifted north and crashed into the European plate. Although this took place on a timescale of tens of millions of years, the results were no less dramatic for that. As Africa pressed against the edge of the European tectonic plate, the layers of rock which made up Europe were driven upwards in much the same way that a rug might be crumpled up if you pushed against the edge of it. The consequence was the formation of the Alps, which rose to a height of almost 15,000ft. For Britain, and in particular the area which would one day be London, the effects were also profound, although perhaps not as visually noticeable as in central Europe.

A large part of what would one day become Britain was still submerged at the bottom of the sea, but very slowly and inexorably, that changed. The sea level rose and fell as indeed did the land itself. Britain was not at that time an island, for much of what is now the North Sea and English Channel were also dry land and connected us to Europe. As Africa continued to push against the European tectonic plate, creating the Alps, something similar, although on a far more modest scale, took place in what is now South East England. Land to the north of London was pushed up, as were the chalklands further south. This created the hollow which now lies between the Chiltern Hills and the North Downs. No river ran through this area yet, for reasons which will shortly be explained.

There have been at least five ice ages, the most recent of which began a little over two million years ago and which, as far as we know, is still going on. Roughly every hundred thousand years, the earth becomes very cold, and the icecaps and glaciers spread south from the Arctic and north from Antarctica. These cold periods are, for obvious reasons, known as glaciations. Then come warmer periods, when temperatures grow milder and the ice retreats. Falling as they do between two glaciations, such temperate spells are called interglacials. This cycle has now been operating for over two million years, with glaciations and interglacials succeeding each other every thousand centuries or so. The most severe of these glaciations is known as the Anglian Stage and it began almost half a million years ago at a time when the River Thames was not at all where we would expect to find it today.

When the great Anglian glaciation began, 500,000 years ago, members of an early human species had visited Britain, but there is no evidence that they came to the Thames Valley; or at least, the Thames Valley as we currently know it. This might be because these early inhabitants preferred to stay close to the water and their remains have been found at the mouth of a wide river which at that time flowed past what is now St Albans and entered the sea where Suffolk and Norfolk would one day be found. The area we now know as London was then an uninviting plain, which was intersected by small rivers and streams, but had nothing in particular to attract visitors. We looked earlier at one of those small rivers, which flowed north from what is now Surrey and left its mark in Essex.

As the glaciers slowly ground their way from what would eventually become the English Midlands, they scooped up rocks and pushed them south, depositing them in, among other parts of north London, the London Borough of Havering. This marked the furthest southern point in the country reached by the ice sheets. It also accounts for the finding of Jurassic fossils in that area today, which have been carried hundreds of miles and dumped with boulders and stones, transported hundreds of miles by the ice. We know to within a few feet how far south the ice sheet reached, and it is because of this that we are able to see too that the River Thames is a relative newcomer to London.

Hornchurch was, until the early part of the twentieth century, a small village in Essex. It has now been engulfed by the sprawling suburbs of the metropolis and is today no more than another district of east London. It was here that a curious discovery was made, about 150 years ago, which allowed us to see when the Thames began flowing along its present course. During the construction of a railway cutting in 1892, a cross section of the geological structure of this part of the Thames Valley was revealed. It was clearly seen that a few feet below ground level was a layer of glacial boulder clay or till. This meant that the ice sheet of the most severe glaciation had reached this far south. A few years ago, during building work a few yards south of the railway cutting, the same thing was found during construction work at a disused gravel pit. On the south side of the pit though, there was no evidence of boulder clay and so we can say with some assurance that the ice sheet extended only as far south as that location.

The most interesting point about the discovery of the glacial deposits in this part of east London though, lay on what was discovered *above* the material which had been deposited here by the advancing ice sheet. This was gravel, Orsett Heath Gravel, to be precise. And although this does not sound especially exciting, the implications are immense.

The River Thames was at one time vastly wider and considerably more shallow than is now the case. The evidence of this may be found in the terraces which run alongside the Thames. As it flowed through the Thames Valley, gravels were deposited on the riverbed. With the passage of time and the lowering of the sea level, combined with the rising of southern England as the weight of the ice bearing down on the north of Britain increased, the Thames cut through its old course and became deeper and narrower, leaving behind a terrace of higher ground, where once it flowed.

This might require a little explaining. As we know, continents are not anchored firmly to the surface of the earth, but float instead upon a sea of molten rock. This is also true of the island of Britain. The ice sheets which covered northern Britian, as far south as London, were tremendously thick. They were over 1,000 yards thick, in fact. The great weight of this ice pressing down on the north of the country, had an effect somewhat like that of a seesaw. As northern Britain was pushed further into the magma which lays beneath the crust, so was the southern part of the island lifted up. This meant of course that rivers would need to flow down a steeper gradient before reaching the sea, which in turn meant that they cut deeper into the earth. This was particularly so, because of all the water which was bound up in the ice which covered so much of the earth. Because so much water was locked up in the ice sheets, so the sea level fell. During interglacials, the whole process was reversed. All of which meant that large rivers like the Thames would at times be broad and shallow and at others swift and deep.

We can see the marks of the alternating sea levels and height of the land in southern England when we look at central

London, where the land around Tottenham Court Road is part of a terrace, which slopes down to Trafalgar Square, which is itself on a lower terrace. From here, the land slopes down again to the present riverbank at Westminster. These terraces may be distinguished from each other by geologists, according to the deposits found.

At Hornchurch, the Orsett Heath Gravel was associated with the oldest and therefore highest of the terraces alongside the course of the Thames. It was laid down roughly 400,000 years ago and was found to overlay the deposits of material which had been brought to the area by the ice sheet. The conclusion was inescapable. The Thames had not flowed through that part of the landscape until *after* the advance of the ice sheet. In other words, 400,000 years ago, there was no River Thames.

It is perhaps slightly inaccurate to say that there was no River Thames half a million years ago. There *was* a large river in what is now southern England, and, like the present-day Thames, it flowed from west to east, but it followed a very different course from that with which we are now familiar. This river, which has been dubbed the 'Proto-Thames' or 'Ancestral Thames', rose in roughly the same place as the Thames does today, but flowed along the line of the Chiltern Hills, passing through the Vale of St Albans to a region of what is now the Suffolk coast, where it entered the North Sea. This was at a time when Britain was not yet an island. As the ice sheets moved south, they eventually blocked the passage of the ancestral Thames and prevented its draining into the sea. The water flowing from the area that we now call Gloucestershire ended up being trapped behind the Chiltern Hills, where it began to accumulate in a gigantic lake. The Chilterns acted as a dam, stopping the water from this lake from escaping. It flooded the plain of Oxford.

After the vast body of water had built up over a period of many years, there came a point at which the water level reached the top of the hills, and it began to overflow into the valley below. This eroded first a notch in the top of the hilly ground, and then a channel. The hills themselves were torn apart as the lake cascaded through the newly formed gap. The torrent of water carried away the chalk and flints of which the hills were made and spread the remains far and wide, as it rushed east across the flat land. In the fulness of time, the entire range of hills was worn away to nothing at that point and the new river, the Thames, was able to flow unimpeded along its now familiar route. The place where the hills once stood is now a valley, along which in addition to the Thames passes the road between Reading and Oxford and also a railway line carrying passengers from London to Oxford and Wales. We know this flat space in the range of hills today as the Goring Gap. Visiting Goring now, it is difficult to equate the gently meandering river which flows past peaceful meadows with this turbulent past.

Nobody was living in the Thames Valley when the River Thames first carved its way across the landscape. Nor was there likely to have been much in the way of wildlife. Further south in Europe, most of the land was tundra, rather like modern-day Siberia, but right by the edge of the ice sheets which covered most of Britain, the ground would be frozen solid for much of the year. It is likely that the new river froze too during the colder part of the year. It would have been a bleak enough environment for any animal to live in and wholly uninviting to humans. Not until the next interglacial began, tens of thousands of years after the formation of the Thames, would people venture north to the area which flanked the new river.

Geology also tells us a lot about the wildlife which flourished in Britain over the millennia. We saw an instance of this when we learned that digging in a patch of sand in South London brought to light sharks' teeth. Obviously, sharks do not now live in the London Borough of Greenwich and so a study of geological formations will give some insight into the fauna of the capital long ago. Just as we now have a clear idea of what the temperature should be in Britain, and we raise our eyebrows at the prospect of its getting a few degrees warmer, so too do we know what animals should be native to the country. In short, a lot of people today seem to subscribe to a view of continuity and a belief that Britain has always been a temperate country, in which badgers and foxes are the largest and most dangerous predators and no land animal is larger than a red deer. We believe that some species are alien and should be eradicated, to preserve the integrity of our ecological system. This short-sighted view of the natural wildlife of the country was common enough 200 years ago, but is today inexcusable.

Until the nineteenth century, most people in Britain took the Bible as being a reliable guide to the history of earth's distant past. That past extended no more than a few thousand years, because theologians studying the genealogies found in the Old Testament had demonstrated that the universe itself had not been created until 6,000 years ago. Using those genealogies and carefully adding up the recorded lifespans of various characters, the seventeenth-century Primate of All Ireland, Bishop James

Ussher, had calculated that the earth had been formed in October 4004 BC. Dr John Lightfoot, Vice-Chancellor of the University of Cambridge and a contemporary of Bishop Ussher's, managed to narrow the moment of creation down even further and established by close examination of Scripture that, 'man was created by the Trinity on October 23 4004 B.C. at nine o'clock in the morning'. Several things caused this perspective to change during Queen Victoria's reign; not least of course, the publication of Darwin's *Origin of Species*. This was not the only event though which made people think more deeply about the way in which the world, and their own country, might actually have been around for a good deal longer than they had previously supposed. It was industrialization which revealed to many people, far more clearly than a book like *Origin of Species*, which few ordinary people had ever read, that their own country had, in the past, been very different. One of the ways that this was brought home with great clarity was the construction of the railways which began to proliferate across the country during the nineteenth century. Railway trains cannot climb very steep inclines and so when hills were encountered, 'cuttings' were constructed, by carving an artificial ravine through high ground. If a steep valley lay on the route, then a viaduct would be built from brick, so that the gradient would be kept as closely as possible to zero. Some of these viaducts required astronomical numbers of bricks. An early example of such a viaduct, which ran from Greenwich to central London, was made of 60 million bricks, and this was by no means exceptional.

Some readers are perhaps scratching their heads at this point and asking themselves what on earth all this has to do with the wildlife of London. The answer is that all the delving in the earth to dig railway cuttings and excavate enough brickearth and clay to produce all those bricks, led to the discovery that the history of the country, and of London, was a lot stranger, richer and more ancient than had previously been suspected. It served also to provide tangible evidence which backed up the ideas expounded in Darwin's groundbreaking book. We saw an example of this with the railway cutting in Hornchurch, which showed that the Thames did not start flowing through that part of the country until after the Anglian glaciation.

Until the Industrial Revolution in Britain, the world was essentially seen as a pretty timeless and unchanging place, which existed now, much as it had been when God created it 6,000 years ago. A quick glance at the cross sections exposed in brick pits and railway cuttings soon gave the lie to such a perspective. It was clear at a glance that both the land and the animals living on or above it had changed dramatically, many times, in the past. The town of Ilford, which is now part of Greater London, provided a good deal of evidence in the nineteenth century of the kind of wildlife which had once been common in this country. Deep pits were dug in the area, because many bricks were needed for building both the railways and also the houses which were springing up in this part what was then Essex at that time. Many remains were found of animals which were either extinct or now lived a good deal further south, in Africa.

In the *Transactions of the Essex Field Club* for 1880 was a paper which perfectly illustrated this aspect of the matter. It was a lecture delivered by a man called Henry Walker and its humorous title was 'A Day's Elephant Hunting in Essex'.

After describing how he and a party of men descended into a brick-pit, Walker said,

> It now begins to dawn on the uninitiated in our party that elephant hunting in Essex, in these modern days, is an underground sport – a recreation restricted to the subterranean world and no longer carried out in the open.

When they reached the bottom of the pit which had yielded up so many bones and fossils, Walker and the others found that they were looking at a vertical wall; a cross section cut through the ground. As Walker said,

> A perpendicular face of the river-bed faces us some seventeen feet in height. Running from left to right until they disappear into the unexcavated ground, and pass away beneath modern Ilford, are horizontal bands of different coloured earths. These successive layers of loam and sand and gravel represent successive changes in the sediments brought down by the old and now vanished river which once flowed over the spot. In fact, we have a lesson here as to how land is made.

The novelty of discovering that elephants once lived in and around London was of enduring interest to many people in Victorian Britain, something which has not changed at all over the years. In 2022, *National Geographic* magazine produced a special edition entitled *Hidden London, Digging Through the City's Buried Past*. Pages 8 and 9 of the magazine feature a double-page spread, which shows an imaginative recreation of the Thames, 124,000 years ago when the shoreline reached as far north as Trafalgar Square. Elephants and lions roam the land, while a hippopotamus wallows in the water. The text reads as follows, 'In a climate of mild winters and warm summers, lions and elephants grazed 125,000 to 24,000 years ago along grassy riverbanks at Trafalgar Square'. It seems that the amusing contrast between the fauna which once inhabited the London area, as opposed to the animals which now live there, is still something which the casual reader finds of interest.

Understanding the geological past in this way, how seas covered what is now Britain, explains the dearth of dinosaur fossils in London and the surrounding areas. Dinosaurs are of course land animals; the large reptiles such as plesiosaurs which lived in the ocean were not dinosaurs. At the time that such iconic creatures as Tyrannosaurus Rex were rampaging across North America, London was entirely submerged and so any reptilian remains from this time will not be of dinosaurs.

In the fullness of time, this part of Britain emerged from the waves and became the home of land animals. These varied dramatically over the years, as the climatic conditions swung back and forth, at one time approximating the modern Arctic tundra and, at others, being similar to the sub-tropical parts of Africa. Because the land was at this time joined to mainland Europe, there was nothing to hinder animals wandering down from the far north or trekking here from Africa. So it was that at different times, lions and hippopotamus have made themselves at home by the Thames, only to be displaced in due course by woolly mammoths. If there is one thing upon which we are likely to remark when looking closely at London's past it is that there has been little stability and that the trees and animals commonly seen at any period offer no clue at all as to what the future might hold. Ice Ages and interglacials follow their own rules, which are wholly obscure to the rest of us.

When the ice sheets, which towered a thousand yards in height, reached as far as north London, practically nothing lived in the London area, other than sparse patches of lichen. It was probably as cold as the present-day Antarctic. Even birds would have found little to sustain themselves under such conditions. As the ice retreated though, the landscape would have resembled something like the tundra of northern Russia. Reindeer were able to graze on the scanty plant life and wolves would have been drawn to prey on them. The only trees were likely to be stunted birch and perhaps pines, scattered across the landscape. It was as the ice retreated further that life in London would have become more interesting.

Because we humans have such short lives, we are unlikely to witness any dramatic change in forestation or climate during our own lifetimes. We might not see much change between our childhood and old age, but that does not mean that we should assume that everything remains stable and unchanging over longer periods. It is this which makes it difficult for us to envisage London in the distant past. Despite all the talk about lions and elephants and tropical oceans, at the back of our mind we still have an image of the temperate environment through which the Thames passes today. Nevertheless, to understand why this part of the world was uninhabited for hundreds of thousands of years, even when much of Europe was populated by our ancestors, we must try and imagine the very different landscape which existed here long ago.

It is time to look at the first people who visited and then came to live in the Thames Valley. To do so, we must cast our minds back almost half a million years and also of course, bear in mind that these first Londoners, as we might call them, did not even belong to the same species that we do.

Chapter 2

The First Londoners

S ome 400,000 years ago, by which time the Thames had moved to its present location, a small band of travellers camped by the south bank of the river, about three miles west of where the M25 motorway now runs. It was a good spot to choose, because in this part of the valley the chalk which lies beneath the Thames Basin rises to the surface and is exposed. This in turn means of course that nodules of flint, that most useful of substances to prehistoric people in Europe, were readily available and simply needed to be prised out of the seams of chalk in which they were embedded. Little wonder then that such a location should prove attractive to the humans who were returning to Britain after an absence lasting many years. This shows us again the importance of geology in early human settlement in South East Britain. Flint being such an extremely important substance to early men and women, it is little wonder that they should wish to spend time in an area where flint nodules may be readily obtained, simply by digging them from the ground.

So handy, from a geological perspective, was the area around the Kent village of Swanscombe, that what was in effect a factory was established here, where flint was dug from the chalk and then converted into hand axes, a typical example of which may be seen in Illustration 6. This activity continued, on and off, for thousands of years. Not only have the stone tools made here been found at this site, it is also where parts of the skull of a woman were found; a woman who belonged to an archaic human species. Before describing the different types of humans around at this time, it might be helpful to describe the area as it would then have been, during the interglacial known as the 'Hoxnian'.

As was remarked in the previous chapter, we have a mental image of what constitutes a 'normal' climate for Britain, one which definitely does not include glaciers or tropical oceans. So too do most of us possess a subconscious template about what animals are natural to the country. This includes of course such things as hedgehogs, squirrels and badgers, but automatically precludes larger and more savage beasts like lions. We know that mammoths and the strange creature known as the woolly rhinoceros roamed the land during the Ice Age, but we seldom think about the fact that while Britain was joined to Europe, the fauna were often more typical of Africa than we might expect in a temperate zone such as that in which we now live.

From examining the remains of animals and plants found in places like Swanscombe, we are able to build up a fairly accurate and comprehensive vision of what the area which would one day become London looked like at that time. The Thames was far broader and more sluggish than it is today. Beavers and dolphins swam in it. On the land, a bewildering mixture of animals lived, some of which are still with us, but others which have not been seen here for hundreds of thousands of years. There were certainly deer, hares and rabbits, as we might expect in this country, but then too elephants came to the waterside to drink, and lions prowled the grasslands which edged the river. The nearby forest teemed with macaque monkeys. It was a strange mixture of the familiar and the wholly unlooked-for.

Turning now to the kind of people who lived intermittently at Swanscombe almost half a million years ago, we remember that until relatively recently, the human family tree was thought to be a very simple, straightforward and linear one. In Africa, arose a special kind of ape called Australopithecus. This then evolved into a species called *Homo erectus*, which was the first human species to leave Africa and explore the world. These early humans spread out from Africa and colonized Asia and Europe. They then evolved into Neanderthals, who in turn became modern humans. Until 30 years ago, this was pretty well the accepted narrative of human evolution. We know now though that it is quite false. For example, modern humans did not evolve from Neanderthals at all; but rather both the Neanderthals and *Homo sapiens*, our own species, arose independently of each other from an earlier species. Neanderthals stand to us in the position of cousins, not progenitors.

Humanity originated in Africa, but the first human ancestors did not venture out of that continent. Most readers will have heard of Lucy, the hominid whose skeleton was found in Ethiopia fifty years ago. She walked the earth over three million years before us, but none of her species ever left the area where they arose. It was not until the emergence of *Homo erectus* almost two million years ago that the human story spread out into the rest of the world. The earliest human remains outside Africa consist of the bones of this species, found in Georgia, on the very edge of Europe. It was to be another million years before humans left evidence of their existence in Britain and even then, the remains are patchy and sparse. Since this book is about the London area, it is not necessary to describe in detail the early forays of humans to Britain.

The current thinking is that *Homo erectus* evolved into another human species, which has been named *Homo heidelbergensis*, and some scanty fossil remains of this species have been found in Britain, dating back half a million years or so. The earliest human remains found near to London though, date from roughly 100,000 years later than this and it is not certain to which species these belonged.

The arctic conditions, alternating with warmer periods, known as interglacials, meant that for thousands of years at a time, the British Isles were uninhabited. For 100,000 years, 125,000 years at a stretch, what we now call the Thames Basin was partly covered with glaciers and the land nearby cold and forbidding. All this changed of course when the ice receded, as it did every 100,000 years or so. It was during one of these warm interglacials that a group of pioneers who were recognizably human camped out on the very edge of that part of the valley which we now know as Greater London, at Swanscombe. This was about 400,000 years ago.

During the summer of 1935, an amateur palaeontologist, whose day job was dentistry, visited a quarry outside Swanscombe called Barnfield Pit. The dentist was called Alvin Marston and while sifting through some gravel, he came across what looked to him to be the back part of a human skull, the occipital bone. He could see that this differed from a modern human skull and so for the next nine months Marston returned regularly to the quarry, to see if he could find any more parts of the skull. His perseverance was rewarded in March 1936, when he unearthed the left parietal bone, which is to say the side of the skull. Despite continuing his search for another three years, those were the only fragments of the skull which the determined amateur could find. It was not until almost 20 years later, in 1955, that two other part-time palaeontologists found the right parietal bone belonging to the skull. With the discovery of this fragment, Bert Wymer and his son John made it possible to piece together a large part of the skull of what might, with only slight exaggeration, be called the first Londoner.

Although the owner of the skull at which we have been looking was known for many years as 'Swanscombe Man', more recent analysis has led to the conclusion that this was a woman, rather than a man, although this is by no means certain. What *is* certain is that on the inside of the occipital bone is a tiny depression known as the *suprainiac fossa*. This feature is found in the skulls of all known Neanderthals, which has led some experts in the field to conclude that Swanscombe woman was a Neanderthal, albeit an early example of that species. This is, however, a minority view. The general opinion is that this is the skull of a member of the *Homo heidelbergensis* group of humans, perhaps at a transitional stage, as they were evolving into Neanderthals.

The attraction of the land which adjoined the Thames at that time is fairly easy to understand and also gives us some idea why so many important modern cities are to be found straddling great rivers. What was so enticing about rivers and lakes to early men and women and why did they seem to gravitate naturally towards them? First, and most obviously of course, is the fact that we all of us need to drink water every day if we are to stay healthy, or indeed even merely to remain alive. In a world without bottles and buckets, with no way of transporting water when embarking upon a journey, it made sense to stay close to a river. There was your drinking water, right there when you needed it. Of course, animals need water too and this is another advantage of being near a body of water; the fact that animals are likely to visit it to assuage their own thirst. This makes riverbanks and lakeshores the ideal spots for ambush hunting, when one remains concealed and waits for the prey to arrive of its own accord, without going out to hunt for it. If one simply hides behind some bushes or trees and keeps quiet, then horses, deer or wild oxen might come to the river to drink, at which point you and your band can leap out and throw spears at them. There is no doubt that the men and women who stayed in this part of the country at that time, making thousands of hand axes, did indeed live on animals which they killed in this way. The bones have been found, dating from this time, with marks of butchery upon them.

Apart from water to drink and land animals to hunt, there were other reasons to prefer a camp near to a river. There are shellfish in rivers, small clams for instance. These can be easily gathered and provide a source of protein. Then too there is wildfowling, otherwise known as hunting water birds. The sort of birds which one sees on land in this country tend to be small, fast and nervous. They are difficult to get close to and even if you *are* able to catch one, there is not a great deal of meat on them. A thrush or a couple of sparrows would hardly make a good meal! The situation is very different with swans, geese and ducks. They spend a lot of their time on the water, and they are larger and plumper than other birds. They do not take flight so readily either and this too makes them easier to catch. Often, they need to run along, rather like aeroplanes going down a runway, before they are able to take to the air. Then of course, there are fish to be caught in the water. It is interesting to note that harpoons or fishing spears have been found in this country, dating back many thousands of years.

The three fragments of the woman's skull which were mentioned earlier are unusual, in that the evidence upon which we mostly rely when it comes to working out what type of people were living in a particular areas hundreds of thousands of years ago consists of discarded tools, rather than the physical remains of their bodies. Fortunately, since these tools are made of a stone which is harder than iron and does not decay or corrode, they are plentiful. Specifically, we are talking here of hand axes. This is an expression which might perhaps need a little explanation.

Illustration 6 shows a typical hand axe from the period of which we are talking, that is to say the Hoxian interglacial. It is about 5in long and shaped rather like a teardrop. Large numbers of these have been found in the west London borough of Hillingdon, and they date from roughly the same period, or a little earlier, than Swanscombe woman; that is to say about 400,000 years ago. The one in the photograph is made from a single piece of flint from which pieces have been patiently chipped away until it forms the desired shape. Flint fractures like glass and, like broken glass, forms sharp edges. The blunt end of this tool fits neatly into the palm of the user's hand, which means that the pointed end can be banged with considerable force at whatever one wishes. For instance, the razor-sharp edges make this a very handy implement with which to cut through the skin and flesh of a dead animal. A more handy device for butchery, it is hard to imagine. The edge can be used to cut a line through the hide, revealing the meat which lies beneath the skin. It is also sharp enough to cut away the sinews and fat and, pounded with sufficient force, it can even break open bones, so that the user can get at the tasty and nutritious marrow within them. This is not, of course, the only use for a hand axe. It can also be used to obtain vegetables to go with the meat. One can hammer through the soil and stones to get at edible roots, the predecessors of our modern root crops.

The hand axe proved so useful to both *Homo erectus* and *Homo heidelbergensis* that it remained in use, virtually unchanged, for a million years. These tools have turned up all over London and indicate that early men and women were finding the area attractive hundreds of thousands of years ago. There is a slight puzzle here, because if this part of the Thames Valley has been so popular, for so long, why was there apparently no permanent settlement here until the arrival of the Romans in 43 AD? This is a question which will be addressed in a later chapter and tells us something very interesting indeed about the culture of those living in this country so long ago. In short, they were happy to exploit the area for hunting and set up temporary bases in London, but there appeared to have been some kind of taboo associated with parts of the river.

The kind of humans who were hunting in Swanscombe and the London area were driven south when the ice returned about 360,000 years ago. Once more, Britain became so cold as to be uninhabitable. When the next interglacial came, it allowed the recolonization of the land, but by a new and different kind of human who was far more similar to us than Swanscombe Woman had been. This was the age of the Neanderthals.

The Neanderthals have had, since the discovery and classification of the first skeleton in the nineteenth century, a bad press, as you might not inaptly put it. Most people believe them to have been brutish, semi-human ape men. We sometimes picture them in our minds as shambling, hairy creatures with low brows and inferior intellects; only one step removed from gorillas and other great apes. This perspective is a by-product of the Victorian idea of an evolutionary 'missing link' between humans and apes. It was thought that the Neanderthals were such a link, being half human and half great ape. In fact, with every passing year, we discover that they were not in any way the inferior of modern humans intellectually and that many of the things which were at one time seen as innovations introduced by *Homo sapiens* when they reached Europe, were no more than improvements on what the Neanderthals had already been doing for years.

One crucial way in which the Neanderthals demonstrated their superiority over the earlier species whom they supplanted was that they had the vision to improve upon the hand axe. This important artifact had, as previously mentioned, remained essentially unchanged for a million years or more. When fashioning a hand axe from a lump of flint, the pieces which are removed are normally regarded as debris and discarded. The flint is whittled away by striking it until it reaches the required shape. The Neanderthals came up with the idea of treating the original piece of flint not as the basis for the finished tool, but rather as the source for many smaller tools. By carefully striking the stone in different ways with other rocks or pieces of deer antler, they were able to knock off substantial flakes which could then be turned into knives, scrapers or spearheads. This activity requires abstract thought. One must have a mental image of the finished item towards which one is working. You must be able to imagine a flake which does not yet exist, other than in your mind and then act upon the external world to bring your idea into existence. After some more shaping, these items could then be glued to wooden handles or shafts. We shall refer again to this topic shortly, because it was in London that the best example of this new process ever discovered in Britain was found. Amazing as it might seem to those who still think of them as primitive and semi-human creatures, little better than apes, the Neanderthals in Europe also discovered how to gather suitable wood and then distil sticky tar from it, which was a perfect adhesive. This was ideal for attaching flakes of flint to arrows or knife handles.

Adhesive was not the only thing which the Neanderthals manufactured. In 2020, the discovery of a small piece of string made from the inner fibres of tree bark was reported from an archaeological site in France. The implications of this were immense, because the fragment predated the arrival of modern humans in Europe. Most vegetable matter from 40,000 years ago simply rots away, but by a miracle, this little bit of three-ply string had somehow survived. String implies the existence of rope, bags, nets and many other artifacts which we usually associate with *Homo sapiens*. It suggests too, mathematical understanding of concepts such pairs and sets. Making string from fibres is a tricky process which requires a good deal of practice. Little wonder then that some of those reporting the finding of the artifact were prompted to say that, 'the idea that

Neanderthals were cognitively inferior to modern humans is becoming increasingly untenable'.

The lifestyle of the Neanderthals did not seem to differ very much from that of modern humans in recent centuries. Like some of the indigenous peoples of North America, for instance, they had a particular interest in the feathers and claws of golden eagles. The Plains Indians trapped eagles and used their feathers for war bonnets. Other parts of the bird were also used to make decorations. Close examination of the remains of eagles dating to the time of the European Neanderthals shows that feathers had been carefully removed and also that attention had been paid to removing claws. Neither activity would have been part of preparation of the bird for food and so the obvious inference is that these parts of the creature were used for decoration.

In other ways too, the Neanderthals appear eerily similar to modern people. They cared for members of their group who were disabled and unable to lead useful and productive lives. One individual, who lived in what is now Iraq, had lost his right arm, was profoundly deaf, had only one eye and could only walk with a limp, and yet had lived to old age with these disabilities. This could only mean that he had been cared for by others for much of his life. They deliberately buried their dead too, together with grave goods. This strongly suggested some type of religious belief, perhaps faith in an afterlife. Then too, they had even begun creating what were almost certainly ritual sites, which also suggests the dawning of religious belief; as does the paintings in caves which are now reliably attributed to Neanderthals. In short, these were people at least as advanced as the *Homo sapiens* who were to emerge from Africa. Indeed, in some ways, they were ahead of *Homo sapiens*.

Only one set of Neanderthal remains have been found in Britain, despite the fact that the Neanderthals were here for so many thousands of years. There may be a lack of skeletons, but there is indirect evidence for their occupation, the best of which comes from London and consists of many stone tools found at a site in Creffield Road, in the west London district of Acton. Neanderthal tools were first found there in the late nineteenth century, but when a school was being demolished in 1974, it was a perfect chance to explore the archaeology of the site in greater detail. There was no doubt that this had been an important place for Neanderthals, because what amounted to a workshop was found, with very clear evidence that the technique being used was what is known as 'Levallois'. This needs a little explanation, although the concept was mentioned above. How on earth is it possible to look at a heap of chipped and broken flint and then be able to state authoritatively that these crude scrapers and blades were produced by one particular kind of prehistoric human, rather than another?

The hand axe shown in Illustration 6 was produced by a member of either the *Homo erectus* or *Homo heidelbergensis* species of archaic humans. A large piece of flint had been chipped away at, until it was the required shape. There was a lot of waste of course and the end-product was just one single tool of a definite shape and design. The Levallois technique devised by the Neanderthals was quite different and this difference can be seen at a glance, even by the untrained eye.

In a nutshell, the best way of describing the Neanderthal method of producing tools, is that it is like a Swiss army knife. Readers will be aware that with a Swiss army knife, one may open cans, bore holes, undo screws or cut paper; they are very versatile devices. What the Neanderthals found was that with a little preparation, a lump of flint could be prepared in a similar way, so that a variety of tools could be produced from a single rock, rather than just one, a hand axe, as had been the case for a million years or more.

A core was carefully prepared by chipping away and shaping a piece of flint. In this way, it was possible to make a rock about the size of a clenched fist from which a variety of things might be struck, with no waste of material. For instance, by banging in the right place, a sharp scraper might be sheared off from the core. Not just one, but a succession of these blades might be obtained, a primitive form of mass production. On the other side, according to how the core had been prepared, it might be that a number of what are known as 'microliths' could be obtained, one after the other, from the same place. In this way, the original core would gradually be reduced, much as a piece of wood is whittled away, but it would be the pieces *removed* from the core which were the tools. In this way, a man might carry around with him a piece of flint which he could use to supply a number of different tools, according to need.

The Levallois method of making flint tools showed how great was the difference between the mind of the Neanderthals and the thought processes of earlier human species. It was now possible for people to have in their minds an abstract idea of a future action and to bring it into physical existence by careful planning, the tool required for the job. Instead of laboriously chipping away at a chunk of flint, so that each blow could be seen, and the results judged second by second as the work proceeded, men could now have a picture in their minds of what might be achieved, even though the object itself was not present.

The workshop in Creffield Road was littered with cores and flakes which had been struck from them. It looked as though this location was, at least for a while, a centre for the manufacturer of flint tools. There is no reason though to suppose that it was part of a permanent settlement. It is unlikely that any of the people working there regarded the area as their home; it was just a staging post as they moved from place to place in search of new hunting grounds. The Neanderthals in London did not put down roots.

Over the millennia, the ice came and went, and the sea level rose and fell accordingly. At times, Britain was a frozen wasteland and then a few thousand years later, it was a warm and hospitable land, with plenty of animals and birds for hunters to prey on. Then came a period when Britain became an island, cut off entirely by the sea from the rest of Europe. And for something like 125,000 years, there were no humans at all, either in the Thames Valley or anywhere else in Britain. The land was deserted and only animals lived there.

We are talking here of such an inconceivably long period of time that it is almost impossible for us to grasp its magnitude. What was happening in the Thames Valley over the course of that time, in the absence of humans?

Roughly 180,000 years ago, the ice returned to Britain with a vengeance, rendering the whole country inhospitable, indeed uninhabitable. The sparse population of Neanderthals fled south and east in search of warmer climes and Britain's climate resembled once more that of the modern-day High Arctic. Reindeer, hares and wolves somehow scraped a living in the desolate landscape for the next few thousand years. Then, with comparative rapidity in geological terms, another interglacial arrived. The ice retreated north, the sea level rose, and Britain became an island. It was an island though without humans. There is no trace at all of any tools or other sign of habitation from this period. There were though plenty of animals and the mix of species was unique; nothing at all like that to be found in mainland Europe at that time.

The summer temperature in Britain during this warm spell was slightly higher than it is now, but only by a degree or two. The climate would have seemed very similar to that which we are used to, but the fauna of the country was very different. It was a strange mix of the tropical and temperate. Some of the animals living near the Thames would be familiar to us now. There were red deer, fallow deer, squirrels and voles, for instance. Alongside them though were creatures which we certainly would not expect to come across in London today.

It has been remarked that there is a fascination with the idea that the Thames and its banks were once home to exotic wildlife more commonly seen in Africa these days than Europe. Of all the animals which might once have lived here, the hippopotamus is among the most improbable and as a consequence, it almost invariably makes an appearance in visual reconstructions of London, as it supposedly was 120,000 years ago. But how did the hippopotamus arrive here?

The ice which gripped the whole of Britain almost 200,000 years ago must have vanished fairly swiftly. We can be sure of this, because no attempts were made by humans to return after the end of glaciation. The earth warmed up and the ice melted, raising the sea level across the whole planet. A minor by-product of this climatic change was that Britain became an island and was cut off from Europe for many thousands of years. It may well be the case that the Neanderthals had sharper wits than we once credited them with and that they were not the brutish sub-humans of popular myth, but there is certainly no evidence that they knew the craft of boatbuilding. The hippopotamus though, needs no boat to navigate the water. After the ice receded, it is likely that herds of these great mammals swam along the coast of Africa and Europe, until they came to Britain. There is no evidence that they lived in mainland Europe at this time though, which is slightly mysterious. Perhaps it was the warmth of the Gulf Stream, flowing from the Atlantic Ocean, which caused them to favour this country. Whatever it was, their bones have been dug up all over Britain, with many being found in central London. Their bones have been found as far north as Cambridge. When they flourished here, roughly 125,000 years ago, the Thames was so wide and high that it lapped against banks which extended as far north as Trafalgar Square.

It is difficult to visualize what London might have looked like at that time. The climate was roughly similar to that which we now enjoy, which is of course considerably cooler than that of Africa, and yet for some reason elephants, lions and hyenas found it agreeable, for their remains too have been discovered in London when digging the foundations for new buildings. How it was possible for fallow deer to survive in a land filled with such fearsome predators is hard to imagine. Deer are very common now in Britain, but this is largely due to their having no natural enemies, other than man. Nothing preys on fully grown deer. That is why the deer population in Britain today is higher than it has been since the Norman Conquest in 1066. The situation was so very different at the time that big cats made their home here and yet somehow, the deer survived. Nor were lions and hyenas the only large and fierce carnivores one the scene. There were bears too to contend with.

At a later date than the time that the elephants and lions were making themselves at home here, conditions changed again and the country became a little cooler, although the ice had not returned. At this time, bears were living in Britain of such a great size that when their bones were first examined, it was thought that they might be those of polar bears. One such creature had its lair at Banwell in Somerset. Two hundred years ago, a local man there called William Beard collected and catalogued thousands of these bones, which he found in a cave. Alongside reindeer and bison were the bones of a brown bear, far larger than those found in Europe today.

Due to the fact that Britain was cut off from the rest of the world for so many thousands of years, evolution was able to produce some oddities. The phenomenon of so-called 'island dwarfism' is well documented. Large animals which are confined to a small area can sometimes shrink over succeeding generations. This can even happen with humans. Most readers will have heard of the so-called 'hobbits' who lived on the island of Flores in Indonesia. This archaic human species was only 3 or 4ft tall, and this small size has been attributed to island dwarfism. Also living on the same island at one time, were elephants which would barely have come up to the level of a modern person's waist, for the same reason. Being a much larger island meant that although Britain was a closed ecosystem, dwarfism had no need to develop; it would not have been advantageous. Instead, some species, like the brown bear, were able to grow to a greater size than usual.

The length of time during which there were no humans at all living in Britain was exceedingly prolonged. If we think back to the conquest of this country by the Romans in 43 AD, we know that this was about 2,000 years ago. Now multiply that by 60 and you have some idea of how long the island was deserted. It was not until the sea level began to fall again, perhaps 60,000 years ago, that people from mainland Europe began to return. Not that it required some special decision on the part of the Neanderthals living there to launch some kind of expedition towards Britain. Britain simply became, in the most natural way, part of Europe, joined to the continent by a vanished area which has been named Doggerland. This occupied much of what is now the North Sea. The remains of Neanderthals and their tools have been dredged up from the ocean floor there.

The millennia wore on, with warm weather alternating with harsher and colder conditions, until about 65,000 years ago things became pretty cold and as a result more water became locked up as ice and the sea level fell. From being an island, Britain was transformed once more into a peninsula, jutting out from western Europe. The North Sea was also dry land at this time and as time passed, men and women roamed into the new territory. These were Neanderthals and for a few thousand years they had the place to themselves. As has been remarked before, this species was a good deal cleverer than was once thought and they were able to survive variations in climate well enough. It was not to last though, because a new human species had emerged from Africa and was slowly, but inexorably, spreading across the world. These were members of our own species, *Homo sapiens*. It did not take long for *Homo sapiens* to replace the Neanderthals and take over Britain. Two explanations are commonly offered for this.

A popular book on science published just before the turn of the present century summed these up neatly,

> It used to be assumed that Neanderthals were simply wiped out by the invaders – certainly a reasonable hypothesis to make in a century which has seen the likes of Adolf Hitler, Joseph Stalin and Pol Pot. Scientists now argue that although the brains of modern humans were slightly smaller than those of Neanderthal's, they were capable of different sorts of activity, particularly in the area of technological innovation.

The idea that *Homo sapiens* outperformed the Neanderthals intellectually and that one species was simply left behind in the race for living space and food by their more resourceful cousins has now become almost an accepted fact for the average person. The dwindling populations of Neanderthals simply could not keep up and *Homo sapiens* were always coming up with new inventions such as bows and arrows which enabled them to survive a lot better than groups who still relied upon spears. There is good reason to suppose that this explanation is too simple to account for what was seen, but since we are never likely to be able to settle the matter conclusively, perhaps we should simply state that it is indubitably true that the Neanderthals who reoccupied Britain after it ceased to become an island, were replaced over the course of time by *Homo sapiens*.

It must be borne in mind that not a single bone of a Neanderthal has ever been found in London, although the evidence for their presence here is strong. After all, bones *have* been found west of London and so it is a reasonable assumption that whoever that individual was, he or she would very likely have passed along the Thames Valley to reach their final destination. Then too, stone tools have been unearthed in London which seem to be typical of those produced by Neanderthals. How did they, and the modern humans who replaced them, exist in the London area as it was at that time?

The last period of glaciation, which we usually refer to as 'the Ice Age' ended about 15,000 years ago. It lasted almost 100,000 years, interspersed with spells of warmer and less harsh conditions. During the colder phases, Britain was like the modern-day Russian Steppes. It was a bleak and uninviting landscape, but somehow, people still lived here. They survived by hunting big game. There was no cunning or finesse about this kind of hunting in open country. It was a matter of groups of men simply following large animals, with no attempt at camouflaging themselves or disguising their intentions. Their prey were creatures which we no longer see anywhere in the world today, animals such as the mammoth and woolly rhinoceros. Both were powerful adversaries.

The mammoth was essentially an elephant covered in reddish or ginger hair. The woolly rhinoceros was a more dangerous version of the more familiar rhinoceros which we see today in Africa. Weighing a couple of tons and with a horn which could grow to over a metre in length, we begin to understand why so many of the human skeletons found from this time show signs of fractures and other injuries which have healed. Attacking such beasts as these with just flint-tipped spears must have been a most hazardous and uncertain enterprise. It wasn't a bit like big game hunting as we understand it today, when a man armed with a rifle with a telescopic sight takes out an elephant from a hundred yards away. This was up close and personal.

Because their hide was so thick, moreover, covered with long, shaggy hair, there was no point in simply hurling spears from a distance. It would be unlikely if any of those primitive weapons would even have penetrated the leathery skins of a mammoth or woolly rhinoceros. Even had they done so, the wound would be more like a scratch or, at most, a shallow cut. Such an injury would be more likely to infuriate a large animal than to inflict a mortal wound upon it. To kill a mammoth, one would need to be very close and to stab hard. Judging by the terrain in which the bones of butchered mammoths have been found, it is fairly easy to work out roughly how such a hunt would have been conducted.

Mammoths, like their close relatives, elephants, are sociable animals. They live in herds. Nobody, even a starving-hungry Neanderthal would probably have been foolish enough to attack a herd of mammoths! The first part of the enterprise would entail separating one animal from the rest of the herd. This in itself would be no easy task. A single mammoth would still present a formidable challenge, even for a large band of men armed with spears. The odds could be improved if their efforts to isolate it could result in its being driven into a marshy or boggy area, where its weight would cause it to be slowed down, as its legs became mired in mud. Some men might have hurled rocks and spears at the struggling creature, but these would be unlikely to kill it. For that, the hunters would have to get in close and jab at the mammoth with their spears, aiming for the heart and head. When one considers the sheer size and bulk of their prey, armed as it was with huge tusks and a heavy trunk, it is hardly surprising that healed fractures are a frequent feature of human skeletons from this time.

Of course, some of the butchered mammoths we find, with cut-marks on the bones, might have been the result of scavenging by humans of animals which died naturally or perhaps fell prey to other predators, but this was not always the case, as the remains found in the west London district of Southall in 1887 show. The skeleton of a mammoth was found, buried 13ft below the street level of the modern city. The archaeologist who examined the remains found something very revealing, which was a flint spearhead, actually touching the bones. This mammoth at least was brought down by human hunters, although whether Neanderthals or *Homo sapiens*, it is impossible to say.

If we wish to know what the life of those people living in and around London at the time when conditions were so inhospitable might have been like, then we cannot do better than to look at how the Lapps, more correctly known as the Sami, manage to thrive today beyond the Arctic Circle. On the face of it, one cannot imagine how these tribes could possibly survive a single winter, there being so few resources to draw upon. Winter in the High Arctic these days gives us a pretty good idea of what London might have looked like at the height of the last glaciation.

The Sami have a symbiotic relationship with the reindeer which they herd. On the one hand, they protect their herds from wolves and other hazards and take care of their welfare. However, they also kill and eat their charges. Both men and reindeer benefit from this arrangement, which has existed for many centuries. It is in the use which the Sami make of their reindeer, both living and dead, which gives us an idea of how life might have been at one time in prehistoric London.

Reindeer provide at least three useful substances for their herders, apart from their meat. The first of these is dung. When you are living on an empty, snow-covered plain, bereft of trees, then you will find the nights very chilly without a campfire. Dried dung burns very well, certainly as well as wood. The Thames Valley at the time of the mammoths would have been littered with the stuff, a 'mammoth' quantity, if readers will forgive an appalling pun. All that was necessary was to gather it up. Since these hunters were nomadic, moving constantly from place to place, there would have been a fresh supply of fuel for their fires every night.

Another substance exploited by the Sami is the antlers of their reindeer. These can be turned into all kinds of useful things, from knife handles to toggles and buttons. Much the same would have been done with the tusks of the mammoths killed by hunters. Ivory was as useful as antler or bone in that way. Mention of bone reminds us just how many uses there were for the bones of a mammoth which had been killed for food. In parts of Russia when the mammoths were roaming, the bones were used to build huts, although there is no evidence of this being done in Britain. Bone though could be used to make needles and harpoons. Fishing was usually undertaken by means of harpoons and bone is the perfect medium for these weapons. Bone can be carved into all sort of useful objects. It is a little-known fact that bone can also burn, if you can build a sufficiently hot fire.

The skins of the reindeer they kill are used by the Sami to make their tents and also sometimes for outer clothing. It is reasonable to suppose that this would also have been the case with mammoth or rhinoceros' skin. Footwear too is usually made of leather. With care, supple leather can be cut into very thin strips and used as thongs, to sew things together. In short, it is likely that bringing down a mammoth would not only provide a huge amount of food for a group, it would also furnish them with raw materials for their clothes, tools and weapons. The example of the Sami shows us how it can be possible, by not wasting anything at all, to scrape out a living in what, on the face of it, seems to be a very unforgiving environment.

No trace has been found in London of the Neanderthals who returned to Britain at this time, although there is evidence in parts of Britain to the west of London. That being so, it is a reasonable assumption that there were Neanderthals in the Thames Valley at the same time that they were in the rest of the country. For 45,000 years or so, the climate of Britain fluctuated, causing it to be deserted at times. For long spells when it was not too cold to live there, the landscape was chilly and uninviting, although hunters eked out a living on the barren land, much as the Sami tribes do today in the north of Scandinavia. We can only guess what was happening in the area of London during those tens of thousands of years. Finally, around 8,000 years ago, the ice had gone, and the sea level reached the present level. Britain was an island and had a permanent population of modern humans, the Neanderthals having by this time died out.

Very slowly, the climate of Britain changed and became warmer. As this happened, the animals and plants slowly began to change and the landscape became more similar to that with which we are today familiar. The mammoths became extinct in Europe by about 10,000 BC and the frozen steppes were gradually transformed into lush, temperate forests. Instead of the willow, juniper and dwarf birch shrubs, which had been the largest plants, taller trees began to colonize the land. Birch trees came first and then pine, which grew into mighty forests.

The growth of the woodlands ushered in a new era, which we call the Mesolithic, and it was to have a profound effect, not only upon the environment of Britain, but also on the way of life, and way of thinking, of those who lived there.

Chapter 3

Hunters of the Mesolithic

By about 9000 BC, much of Britain was covered with dense forests. The London area was thickly forested with lime, oak and elm. There were also pine and birch trees, which had been more common in the colder weather, together with hazel.

The fact that trees were now growing everywhere caused a change in the way of life in this part of the Thames Valley and there is the evidence of two hunters' camps near Uxbridge to show what was happening at that time. Both are in the valley of the River Colne, in West London. One of these sites dates back to roughly 8000 BC and the other perhaps a couple of thousand years later. The earlier of the two camps has the bones of reindeer and horses, which show signs of butchery. The flint blades used for this purpose have been found nearby, together with the cores from which they were struck. It has been possible to fit some of these knives and scrapers back to the cores. All of this suggests that this was the site of a kill and that those who had killed the horses and reindeers nearby, had prepared the meat where the animals had been killed and then carried off what they required to their permanent encampment. The other site had remains of red deer which had also been hunted and killed for food.

It is time to see what life was like in London during the Mesolithic era, or Middle Stone Age as it is sometimes called. Hunting horses and deer is a very different operation from hunting mammoths. The change in tactics must surely have altered the perceptions and ways of thinking of those who now found themselves living in forests, rather than on bare, treeless plains. When your prey is a mammoth, which is a slow, lumbering beast, then it stands to reason that your way of approaching the matter of killing such an animal will be dictated by several factors. In the first instance, finding your mammoth is not likely to require any great foresight or skill. When you live on the steppe, a herd of mammoths is likely to be visible from miles away and so it is only a matter of chasing after them. A running man will be able to catch up with a slow-moving herd, especially if they have young with them. It is then a question of attacking directly with lethal force and hoping for the best, when once you have managed to separate one of the mammoths from the main herd. Hunting deer is another matter entirely.

Anybody who has tried to get close to deer in woodland will know that it is no easy task. They are shy and elusive animals, to say nothing of being well-camouflaged when they are beneath the trees in sun-dappled light. You might catch a glimpse of them, but then again, you might not. Deer are very sensitive to sounds and smells. They have to be, because this is how they evade predators. They are also, of course, exceedingly swift and no man can possibly hope to outpace a running deer. Trying to find a deer in the woodland and then chase it through a forest would be utterly mad.

It was considerations of this kind which led to a change not only in patterns of hunting during the Mesolithic, but also a new way of thinking. Little patience was required during a mammoth hunt, but when waiting quietly for deer or creeping up slowly on a herd of wild horses, patience was needed in abundance. It was a time too when long-term planning began to be vital for survival. Sometimes, an artificial clearing would be made, by chopping down the trees in a forest to form a glade. This is because from the stumps of the trees, new shoots would grow, which would be very tempting to grazing deer. However, those new, green shoots would not appear overnight and so this meant planning for months or even years in advance.

Hampstead Heath is an area of open and uncultivated land which occupies over 700 acres of central London. It is one of the highest parts of the city and it is here that the earliest remains of the hunter-gatherers who lived in London after Britain became once more an island, were found. This period, the time between the peak of the last Ice Age and the arrival of farming as a way of life, is known as the Mesolithic or Middle Stone Age. Bands of men and women roamed the London area, sometimes camping in one spot for a few months, at other times moving from place to place almost daily, in search of food. This was a time when almost the whole of Britain, including most of what is now London, was covered in a vast, primeval forest, known as the 'wildwood'. This wildwood covered most of the land at that time so thickly that it has been suggested that it would have been possible for a squirrel to cross from one side of Britain to another, hopping from branch to branch, without once setting foot on the ground. It is hard for us today to imagine a forest in a temperate country like Britain, which is not managed at all, but simply covers every available bit of land. Even forests which now appear to us to be wild and unmanaged usually have paths of some sort in them. The wildwood was quite different. It was a thick, and in places all but impenetrable, tangle of oak, elm and lime, with hazel and birch forming bushes between the taller trees.

During the colder periods in Britain, the land was more open and the methods for hunting larger animals such as mammoths depended upon simply looking out across the plains for them and then combining together to take one down by throwing spears at it. Now that most places were covered in dense forest and the wildlife was more similar to that which we know today, different methods were required. The largest animals at that time were the great wild oxen called aurochs. There were also red deer. Hunting down and killing such beasts in the woodland was best accomplished with bows and arrows, by hunters lying in wait, rather than a large band of men running straight at the quarry. Finding a deer in a thickly forested areas is no easy matter, even for the experienced hunter. It was at this time that dogs began to be used to help track down the animals and also arrows became the primary means of dealing death, rather than the relatively clumsy spears.

About 7,000 years ago, some Mesolithic hunters camped out on the highest part of Hampstead Heath. They may well have established a semi-permanent settlement here, because the remains of post holes have been found. These indicate that some kind of shelters were built; possibly huts or maybe large tents. These people lived by the side of a small stream, which provided them with fresh water and they manufactured many flint arrows to use in their hunts. They very likely made clothes here as well, which certainly suggests that this was more than just an overnight camping ground. We know this because flint awls have been found, specialized tools designed to bore small holes in leather. Pits were dug and fires lit.

It was the presence of countless flint tools and also many so-called 'microliths' at the site on Hampstead Heath which enables us to build up a picture of what was going on in this part of London 7,000 years ago. Some of the flint tools were designed for making holes in leather, others for cutting and scoring, or to be attached to arrows with resin. The wear patterns on such pieces of stone can often tell what they were used for. Microliths are tiny flakes of flint which were used for different purposes. Often triangular in shape, they could be attached to wooden shafts to make saws or harpoons for hunting fish. It is not difficult to see that animals such as deer were hunted down and killed with arrows, before being skinned. Then holes were probably made in the skin to turn it into either part of a tent or a new piece of clothing.

At Uxbridge, in west London, evidence was found of another hunting method, which was setting fire to reeds and shrubbery in an effort to drive animals out into the open, where hunters were waiting for them. Much of the food which these early Londoners consumed was connected one way and another with the River Thames. On the coast, vast heaps of shells have been found, which suggest that for some living in this country at that time, their diet consisted almost entirely of seafood. Fish spears and harpoons have been found in the Thames from about the same time, indicating that those living inland by rivers also relied heavily upon what they could get from the water. There is good reason to suppose that the area along the shores of the Thames was very important to those living in or passing through the area and not only for practical reasons, but also for what might perhaps be described as religious motives. Before exploring this idea, which will be a recurring theme in this book, perhaps this would be a good point at which to pause and ask ourselves what the people of the Mesolithic looked like. In other words, were they similar to the modern population of Britain? This is not quite such a simple question as it might first appear, because immediately we find ourselves caught up in modern politics and what is sometimes known as 'culture wars'.

The first thing to observe is that each age has a tendency to recreate the past in a particular image. Sometimes this is because concrete evidence is lacking and artists must fall back upon guesswork, at others due to the fact that our own cultural influences inevitably creep into whatever we are producing, whether it is a painting, book or film. None of us are immune to this effect. We see this clearly when looking at artistic representations of the Neanderthals. In the nineteenth century, the concept of the 'missing link' arose. These missing links were intermediate forms in evolution which were missing from the fossil record, for instance a link showing reptiles turning into birds. The idea of the missing link between apes and men became particularly popular after the publication of *Origin of Species*.

When the remains of a Neanderthal were found in the Neander Valley in Germany, after who of course the species was named, it was naturally assumed that this was the 'missing link'. For this reason, Victorian reconstructions show Neanderthals as shambling, hairy creatures, more like apes than humans, often carrying a crude club in the form of the branch from a tree. We know now of course that this a is a gross libel on the Neanderthals, but at the time it fitted in very well with the cultural atmosphere. Looking at artistic reconstructions of ancient civilizations shows us this same phenomenon, in that a picture of ancient Egypt from a children's book in the 1920s has a distinct feel about it of the Jazz Age.

We in the modern world do exactly the same thing with our own representations of the past. For reasons which are too complex to go into here, there is a determined effort today to show that black people were living in Britain centuries, indeed millennia, before the arrival of the *Empire Windrush* in 1948. So it is that television programmes and children's history books now insert images of black people into scenes from the Roman occupation of Britain, as a way of indicating that there is nothing new about Britain's multicultural society.

Over the last few years or so, there have been dramatic, and some would say fanciful, claims about what these Mesolithic hunters in Britain, the men and women who camped out at Hampstead Heath, actually looked like. It has been generally assumed, from the Victorian period up until about seven or eight years ago, that they would have been white Europeans, similar in appearance to those who still visit Hampstead Heath to fly kites or have picnics. Then, in 2018, London's Natural History Museum, in conjunction with a television company making a sensational documentary, commissioned a bust of a famous prehistoric figure, known as 'Cheddar Man'.

In 1903, a human skeleton was discovered in Gough's Cave in Cheddar Gorge, in Somerset. It was later carbon-dated to around 8500 BC, making it the oldest complete human skeleton in the country. Over the years, many visual reconstructions were made, both in pictures and models, which tried to show how this Mesolithic man might have looked in life.

In 2018, Cheddar Man hit the headlines in British newspapers, as a result of a new reconstruction, showing him with black skin. It was said that this must be a shock to racists everywhere, to find that their earliest ancestors were not white at all, but black. The new model sparked debate about immigration, English identity and racism. Even the British magazine *New Scientist* joined in this. On 7 February 2018 it confidently reported that, 'The first modern Briton, who lived around 300 generations ago, had "dark to black" skin.

Two weeks later, *New Scientist* conceded that perhaps there was some uncertainty about the story and that they had been a little hasty, because the geneticists who had actually carried out the work said publicly that the Natural History Museum's reconstruction was purely speculative and other experts asserted that there was no way at all of deciding skin colour on the basis of ancient DNA. A week later, an editorial in *New Scientist* admitted that the television company which had been involved in the affair might have exaggerated the results for their own reasons, saying,

> The whole episode smacks of a publicity stunt to hype up the show. There is some truth in that, but dismissing it outright does a disservice to the scientists. According to the state of knowledge at the time, the genetic analysis did suggest that Cheddar Man's skin was dark. But science progresses, and since the analysis was done last year, many more genes affecting skin colour have been discovered. Understandably, the new science did not make it into the documentary.

In other words, the entire enterprise had owed more to the efforts at which we looked at above, to portray ancient Britain as being full of black people, than it did any kind of objective investigation into the past. Although the bust which was produced showing Cheddar Man in his way is still on display in the Natural History Museum, it is generally agreed today that there is as yet, no possible way of establishing for sure the skin colour of British people who lived 10,000 years ago.

We know that the hunters who lived in London at the time of which we are speaking, that is to say between 9000 and 4500 BC, must have built shelters of some kind, either tents, huts or makeshift dwellings made of branches and so on, but no trace at all has been found of any Mesolithic structures of this kind in London. The faint traces of one or two huts have been found elsewhere, at Star Carr in the north of England, for example, but these seem to have been flimsy and insubstantial structures, rather like lean-tos made of branches and thatch. Because we know that modern hunter-gather groups, among them people like the Khoisan of southern Africa, live nomadic lives, it was always thought that the same would be true of Britain's hunter-gatherers. A moment's thought though will soon show that there is a problem with this perspective.

The old way of life when Britain was cold and joined to the rest of Europe, meant that animals migrated in tune with the seasons and that these movements were connected with things such as breeding patterns and available food. The tribes could follow those migrating herds; indeed, if they felt like it, they could even migrate themselves. If the weather became too extreme, they could head south, as happened when a harsh glaciation took hold. When Britain became an inhabited island, these natural movements of beasts and men came to a halt. When you have an entire continent at your disposal, your options are certainly a lot greater than when you are confined to an island.

The Khoisan of southern Africa, who used to be known as Bushmen, are of course hunter-gatherers. They live in a warm place and can roam wherever they wish. Because the climate is so mild, they need no more shelter than reed mats hung from green branches which have been stuck in the ground. It was something along the lines of this lifestyle that it was once supposed that the Mesolithic people of Britain pursued. It is now believed that their way of life was rather different. For one thing, for a lot of the time, there would not really be any *need* to travel from place to place. If you found a nice spot by a river, then the fish would be there most of the time and so too would the ducks, swans and most other birds. Deer would come and drink and there would be beavers to catch. Once you had a place like that, then there would most likely be a tendency to put down roots, and stay for as long as the food remained available. Then too, there is the small matter of the British climate.

The climate of Britain during the roughly 4,000 or 5,000 years of the Mesolithic period was similar to that which we have today. Readers are invited to consider how likely it would be that a family with babies and young children would be able to survive, let alone thrive, in a hard winter unless they had warm shelter. Tents would probably not do the trick and if a family with children tried to spend the winter living in a draughty tent, then the chances are that one or more of them would have succumbed to hypothermia by the spring. The human body has not changed in the last 10,000 years and the case would have been just the same with a Mesolithic hunter-gather and his wife and children.

At Howick, on the coast of the northern English county of Northumberland, an amateur archaeologist found the remains of a building which has been carbon-dated to 7600 BC. It was a substantial structure, with deep post holes. Several hearths were found, which would have been within the building and in them were the remains of nuts which had been roasted. It was the discovery of this structure and also another at Star Carr in Yorkshire, which caused historians to question the traditional view of the Mesolithic lifestyle. It began to appear that rather than being bands of nomads, wandering across the landscape in search of seasonal foods, some at least of these hunter-gatherers adopted a more settled way of life. It was a discovery in the centre of London, a short distance from the Houses of Parliament, which shed more light upon the matter. Before looking at what was found in the prosaic location of the Thames foreshore at Vauxhall, it might help to consider briefly a site unearthed in Turkey in the 1990s, which caused an earthquake in the world of archaeology and overturned many traditional ideas about the emergence of civilization and the role played in this by the hunters of the Mesolithic.

It has for many years been taken almost as axiomatic that civilization, for example the building of monuments in stone such as Stonehenge and the Pyramids, was a product of the settled lifestyle which agriculture brings. In other words, men and women settle down to farm the land and they then gather together in larger and larger numbers, before starting working communally to erect structures that a single individual or even family would have been unable to manage. All this was thrown into doubt by the discovery of the ruins of Gobekli Tepe in Turkey.

In the mid-1990s, a site in Turkey consisting of massive, monumental architecture was excavated. There were stone pillars with carvings of animals and people, together with walls and enclosures of unknown purpose. This looked at first sight like the evidence for a hitherto unknown civilization which had flourished in this barren landscape. The only difficulty with that idea was that the complex dated back to 9000 or 10,000 BC, at a time before agriculture had begun and people in the Middle East had adopted a settled lifestyle. In other words, this was the product of hunter-gatherers. It looked as though various families must have banded together to build Gobekli Tepe, even though they were not living nearby. Instead of the stone structures being a consequence of people settling down and living together in one place, it was rather the enterprise of constructing the sanctuary or temple which had had the effect of bringing the hunter-gatherers together in a large group. There is evidence that something similar to porridge had been prepared in huge stone troughs, using wild grains which grew nearby. This raises the intriguing possibility that it was gatherings of this kind which prompted the idea of deliberately cultivating grain to provide food for sizeable numbers of people. In short, agriculture might have been a by-product of the building of religious monuments, rather than the other way round.

All this was such a neat reversal of the generally accepted view of the origin of civilization which has been current for many years, that it has caused something of a revolution in the interpretation of ancient history. So it was, that when some puzzling remains were found, submerged for most of the time beneath the waters of the Thames, it was possible to fit them into this new view of the Mesolithic.

On the south bank of the Thames, at Vauxhall, stands the impressive bulk of the headquarters of Britain's Secret Intelligence Service, MI6. It overlooks the river. In 2010, armed police descended upon a small group of people on the foreshore at low tide, as they had been seen setting up a tripod. In 2000, Irish terrorists had fired a missile at the MI6 building and so it was not unreasonable of the police to wish to know what was going on. As it happened, the men and women were archaeologists and they had just unearthed the oldest structure ever found in London. It was not very impressive and consisted only of a group of six wooden posts, each as thick as tree trunks, placed seemingly at random on the foreshore of the Thames. The extraordinary thing about these posts was their age. They were carbon-dated to around 4500 BC, during the Mesolithic era, when only hunter-gatherers were living in Britain. The curious thing about the posts found at Vauxhall was that they were positioned neither in a straight line nor a circle. It was unlikely that they formed part of a building or other structure. It is true that a few huts have been found from this time, but the posts holding them up were nothing like this. It was far more likely that these tree trunks, as thick as modern telegraph poles, formed part of some ritual or religious site. What that might be, could only be guessed at, although there are perhaps clues in both ancient, and slightly more modern, history.

Let us think for a moment about the implications of the size of whatever it was that was built here. Three of the posts were about a foot thick, which is wider than a telegraph pole. The other three were 3in thick, still pretty substantial. Together with these posts were found contemporaneous flint tools, including an adze, used for shaping wood. Let us stop and think for a moment what would be entailed in setting up such an arrangement. It is clear that more than one or two men would be needed for an enterprise of this kind. At least six trees would need to be chopped down and then cut to shape. Branches would need to be removed and the trunk cut to shape, with the roots also be hacked off. Very deep holes would need to be dug. This is a major enterprise for people equipped only with stone axes and adzes. We are assuming, by the way, that those six posts were all that originally existed on this site, which is by no means certain. There may well have been more than six when they were erected.

A site would need to have been chosen and then the nature of the structure decided upon. All this would involve not merely the planning and vision of the finished construction, but also the willing obedience of a workforce. Once the tree trunks have been prepared, then they would have had to be securely implanted in the ground. So securely, that almost 7,000 years later they will still be firmly rooted in the earth, despite tides and floods which now wash over their location. It would be interesting to know if any of our own structures are likely to survive that long!

The posts at Vauxhall only make sense as the product of a community effort, a large group of people who had both the inclination to undertake such an arduous task, that is to say a good reason, and also the ability to organize and direct it. Whatever motivated bands of hunter-gatherers to cooperate in this way for such a project? It is time to examine the significance of the London area in prehistoric times and understand why it became the focus for so much ritual activity over the course of thousands of years.

Before going any further, this might be a good time to mention the concept of continuation of use, which we shall discuss in more detail later on. For now, all that we need to know is that sites of religious significance in ancient Britain, whether burial grounds or shrines, were often established in particular spots which had some tremendous importance which is now lost to us. A couple of examples should make this clearer. Stonehenge was built on Salisbury Plain over the course of more than 1,000 years, beginning in about 3000 BC. Excavations for the nearby carpark in 1966 revealed evidence of an earlier ritual structure, which consisted of holes where hewn tree trunks were erected like totem poles. This work though had been undertaken in about 8000 BC. In other words, 5,000 years before work began on Stonehenge that location was enormously important in prehistoric Britain and when the Neolithic farmers arrived, they continued to treat that part of Salisbury Plain as being somehow holy. The same thing seemed to happen in London.

We can never know what it was which caused certain locations in Britain to be regarded as sacred all those thousands of years ago. The spot on Salisbury Plain where Stonehenge was built has nothing that we can see which distinguishes it from any other part of the plain. Clearly though, 10,000 years ago, groups of hunter-gatherers recognized something here which they felt compelled to commemorate in some way. They did so by doing pretty much the same as was done thousands of years later in London. They chopped down trees, dug deep holes and then erected the tree trunks as some kind of memorial or marker.

One reason that this behaviour seems to us so incomprehensible is that our ideas about the nature of God have changed very greatly since the time of the Roman Empire. All Christians, Jews and Muslims, those belonging to the dominant religions in the modern world, that is, view the Deity as omnipotent, omniscient and omnipresent. By this is meant that we understand Him to be all-powerful, all-knowing and present everywhere and at all times. The conception of God or gods before the time of the Romans was very different and this early idea lingered on in some parts of Europe for centuries. In ancient Europe and the Middle East, various gods were seen as being very much local or, at best, national. The god of Israel, mentioned in the Old Testament was, at least to begin with, a purely national and local god, with power and authority only over the land and people of Israel. It was only later that he morphed into a universal god.

So it was with the gods of Europe at about the same time, they were strictly limited and tended the affairs of particular tribes and regions. These were, if you like, minor gods and goddesses, whose power resided in special locations, where they liked people to worship them and offer sacrifices. Before exploring this theme further though, it might be helpful to think a little about the river which flows through London, the Thames.

The River Thames was of course a very good place to catch fish and waterfowl, as well as providing a good source of drinking water. There was something else which attracted people to the Thames and it had nothing to do with hunting or indeed any material need at all. It was the feeling that this mighty river was in some way holy, perhaps as holy to those living there at that time as the Ganges is to devout Hindus in

India in our own time. For some reason, people felt drawn to the water, not only to obtain food from it, but to make sacrifices.

Many of the things which tell us about the people who lived in and around London thousands of years ago, have been dredged from the Thames. One curious thing which many of them have in common is that they were seemingly both very valuable, but had also never apparently been used. They were, if you like, brand new. Such items range from flint axes to magnificent bronze helmets and shields. Either our distant ancestors were incredibly careless with their most treasured possessions or many of these things were cast deliberately into the Thames. But why, I seem to hear readers asking, would people do something so mad as this? Why would anybody fling something which demonstrated their wealth and importance into a river, where it would have been irretrievably lost? These are fair questions and before examining the idea in detail, we could do worse than examine one or two points; including one from over a thousand years ago and another from the early years of the present century.

In November 2006 a financial marketing agency compiled a report called the 'Fountain Money Mountain'. This revealed that one person in five in Britain regularly throws coins into fountains, wells and other watery locations. This is hardly news, of course, it is simply what many people do when they pass a well or pool of water. The fountains in London's Trafalgar Square and Marble Arch accumulate coins thrown in for luck. When a public fountain or pool is designed, the throwing-in of coins by the public has to be factored into the plans. This may seem so obvious, that it scarcely needs to be mentioned. It is however a very odd way to carry on. Why on earth do we throw coins into wishing wells? This is not a tradition which is unique to Britain. An estimated 3,000 Euros a day are thrown into the Trevi Fountain in Rome. In 2016, this amounted to £1.2 million. This is one modern form of sacrifice associated with bodies of water. It may tie in with some very old stories which have come down to us over the years.

The first written mention of King Arthur dates from the ninth century AD. For the next few centuries, the stories and legends were gathered together, both in Britain and France. The death of King Arthur is treated in a very curious fashion. As he lays dying, the king commands the only knight to remain with him, that he is to take Arthur's famous sword, Excalibur, and throw it into a nearby lake. The story is a strange one, it is difficult to imagine why a dying king would wish his sword to be thrown into a body of water, but this is duly done. There has been, in recent years, what one might describe as a sequel to this story, which may cast light upon the old legend. This is the fact that many swords from the Bronze Age and Iron Age have indeed been found in rivers and lakes. Some of them are in such fine condition, with not a scratch on them, that it is obvious that they were new when they entered the water; they had never been used. The finding of such weapons ties in with the discovery of other special objects, including armour, tools and jewellery, under water. It is unlikely in the extreme that the loss of all these things was accidental; it is far more likely that they were cast into rivers and pools as some kind of sacrifice. The River Thames was almost certainly an important location for the making of such sacrifices and this is a tradition which has lingered on in this country right up to the present day. These days, our offerings are purely nominal, in the form of a coin or two, but the essential nature of the activity has remained unchanged for at least 6,000 years.

Rivers, wells, pools and bogs were seen as gateways to the underworld; the world of the dead and also the gods. It was probably thought that gifts deposited in such places would find their way to this supernatural realm. A curious echo of this belief which persists to this day in London is worth mentioning, for it shows that folklore of this kind lingers on in the modern world.

During building work at Southwark Cathedral, which stands near London Bridge station, a well was uncovered which dated backed to the Roman occupation of Britain. Carved statuary had been placed in the well, stone images which included that of a British god. This was of a young man, wearing a Phrygian cap, with a quiver of arrows carried over his shoulder and accompanied by two animals. He appears to be a hunter. It is likely that these had been placed in the well as offerings or sacrifices to the gods who supposedly dwelt beneath the ground. In another part of the cathedral, excavations revealed a Roman road which ran nearby and also a stone coffin. The coffin was left on display at the bottom of a shaft which was four or five yards deep, with a barrier so that the curious could peer down to the original ground level of London, as it was 2,000 years ago. No sooner had this arrangement been put into place than the tribute of coins began. This was no fountain or wishing well, but it was certainly a route down to the world of the dead, as symbolized by the empty sarcophagus. So many coins were thrown down onto the coffin that it began to be scratched and chipped. Eventually, the authorities in the cathedral were obliged to put a sign at the bottom of the shaft, telling people not to throw coins down. In such a way, ancient customs are maintained. The coffin and the notice asking people not to throw coins down into the world of the dead, may be seen in Illustration 7.

In other words, that part of the country which is now central London had some kind of religious or ritual significance to people living in and around the Thames Valley and this belief was present as early as the Mesolithic era, as is suggested by the posts at Vauxhall. Perhaps thinking a little more about the idea of wooden posts which are regarded as being in some way special or holy might help us understand both the site which we have been considering and the nature of such places in general. Scattered across Britain in the Neolithic Age and Bronze Age were various sacred sites which featured wooden posts or poles. On Salisbury Plain there is Durrington Walls and the monument known informally as 'Wood Henge'. On the coast of Norfolk, a circle of wooden posts dating back 4,000 years has been found. Nearer to London, a henge composed of wooden posts was unearthed at Shepperton, not far from the film studios. An enclosure of banked earth and chalk was connected to the nearby River Ash by an avenue of wooden posts, very similar to those found at Vauxhall. Shepperton though was built a thousand years later. It is likely that the site at Vauxhall is part of the same general tradition. Just what that tradition entailed is not clear.

There are very ancient mentions of what are described in the Bible as 'sacred poles'. Stone pillars, which are sometimes assumed to be phallic symbols, are found in many places and these may be more permanent representations of wooden poles. Chapter 31 of the second book of Chronicles in the

Old Testament tells us that the people of Israel broke the stone pillars associated with other religions and tore down the altars and 'sacred poles' which they found in the high places belonging to nations and tribes which they supplanted from the promised land. Although we have no written records relating to the wooden poles erected during the Mesolithic and Neolithic periods, we can perhaps glean some idea of what they were meant to represent by looking at a more recent episode in history, one dating back to the time of Charlemagne in the eighth century AD.

In 722 AD, King Charlemagne raided and destroyed a pagan site of worship in what is now Germany. This was a location where Saxon tribesmen worshipped a carved tree trunk which they had set up in the middle of a forest clearing. Wooden totem poles of this kind were known as irminsuls, and it was thought that they represented the Ash Yggdrasil tree, the World-Tree of Norse mythology, whose roots were in the underworld and whose crown reached the heavens. Something of this sort might very well be a continuation of the Mesolithic and Neolithic custom of erecting tree trunks at special spots in the landscape. It has even been suggested that this practice continued within living memory and that the ritual of dancing around the Maypole on May Day is a faint echo of fertility rites which were practised in some agricultural communities. It must be borne in mind that May Day is none other than the Celtic festival of Beltane.

There is also the interesting example of the oldest three-dimensional representation of a human face ever found, which also dates from the Mesolithic, and is carved in precisely the same way as a totem pole of the Native Americans. In 1890, a strange wooden carving was unearthed from boggy ground at Shigir, a remote part of Russia, hundreds of miles east of Moscow. It consisted of a crudely depicted face at the top of a pole which was decorated with geometric patterns, combined with other representations of human faces. This object had to be extracted in pieces, so deeply was it embedded in the ground and when the various parts had been assembled, it was obvious that this was originally a tall, thin pole, surmounted by a human head. It is only since the advent of carbon dating that it has proved possible to say with any certainty just how old the Shigir Idol, as it was named, actually is. It is was made from a tree which was felled roughly 12,000 years ago, around 10,000 BC.

It is impossible now to say what the purpose of this carved pole might have been. It has been calculated that it was originally over 16ft long, which makes it fairly certain that the base would have been buried in the ground, so that the decorated portion would tower above people. Various suggestions have been made as to what it meant, but there can be little doubt that at one time, it stood upright in the ground, just like the wooden posts which have been uncovered at Vauxhall.

Combined with the very strong likelihood that some kind of ritual sacrifice of material objects was being undertaken on the bank of the Thames in prehistoric times, it is probably a fair guess that the posts found at Vauxhall were of religious significance, rather than having any practical purpose. A wooden idol, similar in some ways to that found at Shigir, was dug up in east London in the 1920s and found to date from the end of the Neolithic, and we shall examine this in a later chapter. For now, it is enough to say that for perhaps 5,000 years, hunter-gatherers lived in the region of the Thames which we now know as London, and that in addition to scraping a living by scavenging and hunting, they also engaged in religious practices which centred around the river. Just what this religion consisted of, we cannot say. However, when farmers from the east arrived in the area, around 4500 BC, they brought their own religious beliefs with them, but rather than imposing them upon the people whom they found here, they adopted some of the rituals which they encountered. Chief among these was reverence for the mighty river which flowed through the territory.

Choosing Vauxhall as the location to erect those posts was not a random act, but to understand why this spot on the river might have been the ideal place for hunters of the Mesolithic to mark in such a fashion, we need to go back in time and think about the Thames not as it is now, but as it was thousands of years ago. Of course it was a good deal broader and more sluggish than it is today, because it was not confined between high stone walls. Another point to remember is that various smaller rivers and streams flowed into the Thames from both north and south. Illustration 8 shows some of these rivers, the courses of which can still be traced today, although the rivers themselves have long vanished underground.

At the point where those tree trunks were planted deep into the bank, two rivers met, and their combined flow had an effect upon the nature of the Thames in this part of the valley. Travelling upstream from the estuary, when the Thames reaches Westminster, the river makes a sharp turn to the south and then a few hundred yards later, it makes another right angle as it resumes its course west. Two rivers enter the Thames in this section. From the west, the Tyburn divides and forms a delta, with two branches entering the river; one south of Parliament and the other just beyond Vauxhall Bridge. Right by the bridge, the Effra flows into the Thames from the other bank. This confluence served to make the stretch of the Thames between Westminster and Vauxhall bridges special in several different ways.

The first point to remember when trying to work out why the area of central London might have been so significant for people living in Britain all those thousands of years ago is that the tidal head, that part of the river which rose and fell with the tides, extended to the bend in the river at Westminster, but no further. The river up to this point was brackish, which is to say that it was a mixture of fresh water and salty. This was also the first point at which it was possible to ford the river.

The fact that the part of the river into which the Tyburn and Effra flowed was completely fresh and that this state of affairs changed abruptly at the ford, would have been important to those early people who were familiar with the area. What are known as 'liminal zones', that is to say places on the border between two different kinds of space, were of great importance to early Europeans. These might have been riverbanks, seashores or, as in this case, the point at which brackish and salty water miraculously become sweet and pure.

Crossing points of rivers, whether fords or bridges, have traditionally been places connected with magic and the supernatural. Bridges often had sacrifices made when they were constructed, to ensure the safety of those passing over them. We see echoes of such beliefs in our folk history. Most readers will be familiar with the peril faced by the three Billy Goats Gruff when they wished to cross a bridge, for a malevolent spirit had taken up residence beneath it and those crossing were in danger from this entity.

The conjunction of ford, fresh and brackish water and the point at which three rivers met, would all have worked to make this stretch of the Thames a special location. It was a 'liminal zone', in other words a border where one thing changes into another. Liminal zones may be spatial or temporal. The shore is a liminal zone of course, where the land becomes sea, and twilight is also such a zone, the border between light and dark. The stretch of the Thames where the Mesolithic posts were found is a liminal zone in several senses. The rivers Effra and Tyburn cease to be separate entities as they merge with the Thames between Westminster and Vauxhall, although there would have been no sharp division, as both rivers would have had wide estuaries at this time. This is one liminal zone. There was likewise no clear demarcation between the brackish or salty water and that which was fresh and potable. That too was a liminal zone.

Before going any further, it might be as well to admit at once that nobody knows anything about the religious beliefs of the people who lived in the London area before the establishment of the Roman city. All that we can do is offer speculation and conjecture. This is what has been done about the posts found on the Thames foreshore at Vauxhall. Other groups of wooden posts from roughly the same time have been found elsewhere in the country, at Stonehenge to give one example. We really have no idea what they represented or why they were erected. It is important to emphasise this point now, because in the next chapter we shall be looking at what is sometimes called a 'ritual landscape' in and around London and trying to work out the significance of what remains.

Read any book about prehistoric life in Britain and you are sure to encounter endless qualifications and modifiers.

Such and such an activity, was 'possibly' connected with ancestor worship, this site 'might' have an astronomical purpose, the deposition of bones in a hole is 'perhaps' part of a religious ritual. To see why it is all but impossible to read the minds of those who lived thousands of years ago, before the development of written language, it will only be necessary to cite two instances of practices around the disposal of the dead; one from this country and the other from Scandinavia.

Something striking about the way in which human corpses were treated in Mesolithic and Neolithic Britain, and also later in the Bronze Age, is that human remains were not simply buried in one place and then left in peace. In passage tombs, a type of long barrow, the bones were constantly being moved around and rearranged, for reasons which we can only guess. At Bela Knap, a long barrow in Wiltshire, are the remains of thirty-one people who were interred thousands of years before the Romans conquered Britain. The bones have been carefully placed and moved about. One skull has had finger bones carefully inserted into the nasal cavity. Obviously, this was done for a special reason, but what that reason might have been, it is quite impossible for us to say today. In Sweden, an even more peculiar discovery was made in a tomb from the Neolithic, which consisted of a human ankle bone which had had four holes drilled through it. Into these carefully fashioned sockets, had been placed four human teeth. It is literally inconceivable to any person in the twenty-first century, that somebody would meddle with human remains in this way, but it clearly meant something to whoever undertook this task.

We must remember this when we start to look at some of the mysterious structures which have been found in the London area, such as the causewayed enclosures and the strange ditches and banks running for miles across the landscape that we now call a cursus. The number of theories about the meaning and purpose of such things is unlimited, but when all is said and done, none of us can really say what was going through the minds of those who put such a tremendous amount of planning and work into building those monuments.

The Mesolithic way of life lasted for in Britain for over 4,000 years. The people who lived along the Thames Valley did not leave any trace of their activity, other than the poles at Vauxhall, the remains of a few campfires, and the detritus of their flint knapping. Those who followed on though, and invaded and occupied this island during the Neolithic, the Bronze Age and the time of the Romans, adopted some of the places which were special to the hunters. Why, we do not know, and nor do we know how those who came afterwards could tell where those special places were. In the depths of Epping Forest, which was at the time of the Mesolithic part of the great forest which covered practically the whole island, some Mesolithic hunters had a campsite which they used regularly. Five or six thousand years later, Iron Age warriors built a hill fort right by this campsite. Was this purely coincidental or was there some religious or supernatural reason for choosing the same spot for the fortification as that previously used by those who had lived here so long ago?

This reuse or appropriation of certain locations is something we see time and again in London, with the importance of some spots being recognized even by the Romans when they arrived here. At Harlow, in Essex, for instance, a Mesolithic site was subsequently used during the Bronze Age, following which an Iron Age temple was established there. When the Romans arrived, they built a temple of their own on the spot and when the Saxons later took over this part of the country, they too venerated that particular spot by the Rriver Stour. This meant that for 5,500 years, one small patch of ground had somehow maintained its sanctity.

Around 6,500 years ago, the landscape of Britain, the way of life and the very people who dwelt there, changed abruptly. The day of the Mesolithic hunter-gatherers who eked out a living by the Thames, came to an end, and a new era dawned. This was to be the age of farming or, as it is more commonly known, the Neolithic or New Stone Age.

Chapter 4

The First Farmers and the
Ritual Landscape of London

It was for many years accepted more or less as fact that farming began in that part of the Middle East known as the Fertile Crescent and that it gradually diffused outward from there, across the world, until eventually the practice of agriculture reached Britain. This version of history had the merit of being very straightforward and easily understood by pupils studying history at school. The only disadvantage of this simple and coherent narrative is that it is almost certainly false. The modern view is that agriculture arose independently, at various times, in a dozen different parts of the world, ranging from India and China to both North and South America. This does not however materially alter the origin of farming in Britain, for it remains the case that whatever was happening elsewhere in the world, it was farmers from the Middle East who exported the practice to Europe, from where it reached Britain, something over 6,000 years ago.

Although the evidence is clear that farming appeared in Britain around 4000 BC, there was for many years a debate about whether it was farming or farmers which arrived across the English Channel. In other words, was this a new culture, a new way of doing things, which the people living in Britain somehow picked up from those engaged in agriculture in Europe, or was it a migration of new people, who would eventually supplant the hunter-gatherers who were living in the country at that time? Until fairly recently, the balance of opinion in orthodox circles tended towards the idea that farming was an idea, one which was brought to this country. British people, by this reading of the situation, would have been in touch with Europe and seen the advantages of a settled existence and acquired from those living in Europe both wheat seeds and domesticated goats and sheep. Advances in genetics, though, have settled this debate quite definitely. Six thousand years ago, waves of immigrants arrived in Britain, people whose heritage lay in what is now Turkey and Greece, and they brought with them a way of life which would transform the British Isles, physically and culturally.

The replacement of one population in Britain by another was not a rapid and bloody affair. We should not think of those early farmers sweeping across Europe from the east, and exterminating the hunter-gatherers whose lands they were usurping. It was an exceedingly gradual process. Agriculture took a couple of thousand years to reach us from the Middle East. On the way here though, something unfortunate happened, which was to have a bad effect in the long run when farming finally became established in this country.

When the first farmers began moving west from Anatolia, the central plateau in what is now Turkey, they brought with them a variety of crops. At the Neolithic village of Catal Huyuk, for example, on the Anatolian plateau in what is now Turkey, six cereals and seven pulses were being cultivated, 7,000 years ago. Gradually though, as the farmers spread out from this area and settled in Europe, satellite communities grew up over the centuries as agriculture became more and more the way of life in Europe. By the time the farmers reached Britain, only one or two types of plant were sown; those which were found to grow reliably in the cooler climate of Europe. To begin with this, this did not matter all that much. It is quite possible for a large territory to thrive by planting only a single type of root or grain. One need only think of the way in which Ireland subsisted for many years by growing almost nothing but potatoes. We all know what happened though when a disease infected the potato crop in Ireland during the nineteenth century. It was a disaster, which resulted in a terrible famine. This is always a hazard when you rely only upon one or two crops. The failure of a harvest can be disastrous.

The Neolithic farming revolution was therefore a chancy and uncertain business from the start and seemed to operate rather on a boom-and-bust cycle. When there was good weather and the wheat flourished, all was well. People had sufficient food, and their numbers increased. However, some blight might affect the fields or there would be a poor harvest because of a cold and damp year and then the farming communities would go hungry. This could lead to a reduction in population. Sometimes a pest would cause a catastrophic failure of crops and this could, for people wholly dependent on just one or two types of plant, be a very serious matter. In some ways, agriculture was an improvement on the life of the hunter-gatherers, but there were disadvantages. This agrarian lifestyle, based on the growing of crops, eventually gave way in some places to pastoralism, in which the focus is more on livestock.

Britain was by this time an island and it would remain so right up to the present day. The distance across the ocean though was not a daunting one and could easily be crossed by makeshift rafts, rather than there being a need for sophisticated vessels. This meant that the farmers from Europe had no difficulty crossing the English Channel and bringing with them their new way of life.

Those arriving in Britain set out to change the landscape. There were two motives for doing so; one practical and necessary and the other, at least to modern ways of thinking, less important and relating to religious beliefs. This is though, as we shall see, a wholly artificial division. For those who arrived at this time, there was no essential difference between material and spiritual needs. These two urges worked in tandem to produce what are now known as 'ritual landscapes'. There is good reason to suppose that what is now London was at one time just such a location, that is to say a large stretch of open country which had some particular significance to those who lived thereabouts. We saw in the last chapter that even before the arrival of the farmers, those living near the Thames had been building what were probably religious structures and making sacrifices to the river, by casting stone weapons and tools into it. The newcomers accepted this reverence for the location and incorporated it into their own belief system.

The people living in the country at the time that farming arrived had no motive for cutting down trees, although they did so occasionally in a small way. Sometimes, clearings would be made, so that new shoots springing up from tree stumps might attract deer to graze upon them. These would then be ambushed. Other than that though, there was simply no reason to expend energy on such an arduous and time-consuming business as forestry. After all, the forest covered almost the entire island of Britain and it would make little difference to hunter-gatherers if it remained or were to be cut down. The case is greatly altered though, when you wish to establish a farm.

London was, like almost everywhere else, part of this great forest. The area around the Thames was not so thickly covered with trees, because it was marshy and subject to regular flooding. This is a strange thought today. Walking around central London in the twenty-first century, the whole area is as dry as a bone. The single river which cuts the city in two is very clearly demarcated and does not venture beyond the stone walls which encompass it. None of the other rivers which flow through London are visible, having long ago been culverted over and driven underground. You will not catch so much as a glimpse today of the Walbrook, Fleet, Effra, Westbourne or Quaggy River. At the dawn of the Neolithic period though, the city presented quite a different appearance. The centre of London was a network of rivers and channels, surrounding islands; some of which were almost flooded at high tide. The scene would have looked very much like the Norfolk Broads or perhaps the fenland of East Anglia before it was drained. Illustration 9 gives some idea of what Southwark might have looked like at that time. The evidence suggests that farming took longer to become established here than in the drier areas.

The first indication of farming in the London area is from about 3800 BC. Hampstead is on high ground, a few miles north of the Thames. A site investigated there revealed that the tree cover had been removed, that is to say the trees of the wildwood chopped down, which had allowed cereals to grow, along with plants like mugwort. It was with the coming of the farmers that stone axes became an important, indeed essential, tool in Britain. Trees would be hewn down over an area and then probably burnt. The tree stumps would have been impossible to tackle with the technology then available and so would have been left to rot away naturally. Crops would have been sown in the land between the stumps.

This method of clearing woodland for the planting of crops is sometimes known as slash and burn. Even if the population of an area does not increase substantially, slash and burn becomes an expanding process which will, in the course of time, result in widespread deforestation. This is because those who undertook the process thousands of years ago had little idea of the science which underpins efficient farming. When first you clear a patch of woodland in this way, the land is likely to be full of nutrients, from all the leaves which have over the years fallen to the ground and decomposed. After you have sown and reaped crops there for a few years though, all the minerals will have been used up. and without fertilizers, the soil will become barren, unless it is left fallow for a while. The answer is of course to cut down another section of forest and repeat the process there. In this way, thickly wooded land is transformed over the course of years into open country.

There was at the time of which we are talking, no question of cities being founded or even small towns. Instead, individual farms and homesteads were the order of the day, rather like those in the United States as the west of the country was opened up to settlement in the nineteenth century. The settlers in Britain preferred high ground, near springs of fresh water, rather than the area immediately next to the Thames. There was good reason for this, because the land near the river was soggy and crisscrossed with channels and small rivers which ebbed and grew with the tide. The water was brackish and muddy, rather than the clear water which flowed from little streams further from the Thames. There is reason to suppose that the indigenous hunter-gatherers, lingered on around that part of the valley, continuing to eke out their living and shunning the new way of life which the invaders had brought with them. There is no evidence of outright fighting or violence between the two groups. In the course of time, the farmers simply came out on top because their lifestyle brought with it better health and less chance of starvation.

Little by little, the wildwood was forced to retreat from where London would one day arise. It was not the work of a few generations, but rather a process lasting for centuries. As the trees were hacked down and the stumps rotted away, so a patchwork quilt of little fields slowly but inexorably expanded, pushing back the dense forest. Although there is occasional direct evidence for the farms which were appearing at this time in London, much of what we find must be carefully studied and analysed, before we can work out what lifestyle was being pursued. An excellent instance of this process of induction is to be seen when looking at some of the remains unearthed in east London when a new headquarters for the multinational company Amazon was being built in 2015.

Shoreditch is part of London's East End. A stream called the Walbrook once flowed through this area, although it vanished underground long ago. A little over 5,500 years ago, this area was home to an agricultural community. These were farmers whose ancestors had crossed the English Channel and settled here three or four centuries earlier.

Part of the new way of life which was introduced to this part of the country during the Neolithic was the use of pottery vessels for storing food in and cooking. Hunter-gatherers seldom need such things, for they moved to where the food they required was to be found and then ate their fill until it was time to move on in search of somewhere else to camp. Meat from the kills which they made could easily be roasted over a fire and there was no need for any pots to store it in. Even today, people following this way of life move around a lot and carrying heavy clay jugs and bowls would be a needless burden. The case is very different for farmers, who are living in the same place for years on end. They need vessels to store seed and grain, and also to keep butter and cheese in if they are keeping flocks of sheep and herds of cattle. The weight of such things presents no difficulty, because they are stored in their homes, rather than having to be carried about from place to place.

Archaeologists from the Museum of London were allowed to examine the site in Shoreditch of Amazon's new building, as the foundations were laid and before construction began. They found a large cache of pieces of broken pottery, almost 500 fragments which proved to belong to 24 separate items. Some of these had been decorated both by fingers being pressed in the wet clay as they were being made and also by using a deer's hoof to make pleasing patterns. Very little Neolithic pottery had previously been found in London and so there was determination to wring every scrap of information possible from these unpromising bits of broken pots and jars.

At the University of Bristol, a new technique was developed for extremely accurate dating of the potshards, and this revealed not only when they were made but also some fascinating information about the lifestyle of those who had used these vessels. This entailed extracting food residues which had seeped into the porous and unglazed surfaces of the pots, and then using radiocarbon dating on these fatty substances. The results were astonishing. It proved possible to pinpoint the date that the pottery was in use to 3600 BC, give or take 70 years either side of that year. This placed them firmly in the first few centuries after the arrival of agriculture in Britain. There was however much more to be revealed by the analysis than simply the age of the food with which the pottery had been in contact.

Some of the fats extracted from the clay were from milk products, including butter and cheese. These had been produced from the milk of cows, sheep and goats, which immediately indicated that the land near to where the pottery had been excavated was used for the keeping of domestic livestock; in other words, this part of London had at one time been farmland. The remains of fat from mutton and beef were also found, but not pork fat. One possibility was that there was some taboo on the eating of pigs, as has been common throughout the Middle East for thousands of years. The eating of pigs is of course prohibited by both Islam and Judaism.

Since we can be sure that farmers were living in central London almost 6,000 years ago, what sort of homes did they have? Many of us have a vague idea that ancient British people lived in roundhouses until the time of the Roman invasion, but actually roundhouses were a later development, which became widespread during the Bronze Age. The houses which have been found in and around London, which date from the Neolithic, are very different. For one thing, they are much bigger than the houses in which the Britons were living when Julius Casar landed in 55 BC. For another, they are a different shape.

At Runnymede, which is a short distance from London and famous of course as being where King John affixed his seal to the Magna Carta in 1215, an archaeological dig in 1989 found the remains of the earliest house yet to be discovered in the Thames Valley. Although the structure itself had long rotted away, being composed of wood smeared with plaster or dung, it was possible to trace the outline from the rubbish which had been discarded along the outside walls. Pieces of broken pottery and flakes of flint had built up into little mounds and showed that this had been a large house and probably functioned as both living quarters for humans and a barn for livestock. Postholes were found which were all that remained of the stakes which had at one time formed the basis of room dividers. Pots were also recovered from the site and found to contain traces of honey. This suggests that as early as 3000 BC, beekeeping might have been practiced in the London area.

What was most noticeable about the house was that it was rectangular. The outlines of other houses from this period in other parts of Britain confirm that this was the general pattern for Neolithic houses in this country. They were more roomy than some of the later roundhouses, but this was because they functioned too as barns. Animals and humans shared the same living quarters, an arrangement which was far from ideal and led to the spread of disease.

Gradually, those parts of the country which were not used for farming also began to be exploited for their potential, including what is now central London. The previous inhabitants had camped out and hunted by the Thames. Some of the places where they were based for their activities are still remembered in the names of certain districts which lie by the water's edge. Where some of the many little rivers flowed into the Thames, gravel islands had formed. These were convenient spots for hunters to lay in wait and in Saxon times they became known as eyots. These islands are no longer visible, but they were prominent locations in London as late as medieval times. Riverside locations with names ending in 'ea' or 'ey' indicate that they were named after such eyots; Bermondsey, Chelsea and Battersea being good examples. Although to begin with the land by the Thames in central London was not cultivated by the newcomers, they gradually displaced the hunters who had been using the area. Just as they had modified the forest to provide space for their farms, so the men of the Neolithic tamed the boggy land next to the great river and made it a little more convenient for their purposes.

This was the first way in which the farmers of the Neolithic changed the landscape. By cutting down forests and planting crops, they altered the appearance of the land. Sometimes though, the sculpting of the environment was a by-product of other activities, such as fashioning paths through woodland, in the later part of the Neolithic. Until the arrival of agriculture, humans did not really cause any changes to the appearance of the landscape in the Thames Valley. Mesolithic hunters might from time to time have cleared small glades in the woodland, in order to promote new growth of young trees, to attract deer, but that was all. Otherwise, they moved across the land, taking what they needed and leaving little behind, other than their footprints.

This changed dramatically once the Neolithic farmers arrived. For them, the landscape of this part of the Thames was a raw material upon which they would work, remodelling according to their wishes and desires. This was partly a natural consequence of the introduction of agriculture, and also undertaken as a religious activity, a concept at which we shall shortly be looking, but then too there were unlooked-for consequences of their activities, such those which resulted from the construction of trackways and paths. It is possible to see the evidence for such incidental changes to a forest today. Incredible as it might seem, a Neolithic track still exists, one which may be walked along and has been in continuous use for over 4,000 years. Most amazing of all, this remote fragment of a long-vanished era is just three miles from a London Underground station!

Most people have heard of the so-called Sweet Track in Somerset. This is a wooden trackway which ran across marshes and allowed those in the area to move from place to place easily. Since the discovery of the Sweet Track in 1970, many more similar causeways have been found, including a number in London. The oldest of these was unearthed during the building of Belmarsh Prison in south London. Radiocarbon dating showed that it was around 6,000 years old. An earlier discovery in Silvertown, on the other side of the river in the East End, was of a trackway which was 700 years younger than that at Belmarsh Prison. In fact, the whole of east London, on both sides of the Thames, appears to have been crisscrossed with such paths. It has been estimated by researchers from one museum that there could have been 1,100 miles of such paths in the outer London boroughs such as Redbridge, Havering and Barking and Dagenham alone. We shall explore this possibility in a later chapter.

The structure of these paths was simple, but very effective. Stakes were driven into the soft, spongy ground and these were used to support planks of wood, which lay on branches and twigs which had been scattered on the ground. To make the planks less slippery in the wet conditions, moss and twigs were strewn across them. Such tracks meant that travellers were able to make their way along the edge of the river more easily. That these pathways were established right on the edge of the water and passing through the marshes, tells us that people were living close to the Thames and wished to move from one part of the foreshore to another. There is of course higher, and drier, land, just a few hundred yards from the water's edge. Thinking about the trackway found near Belmarsh Prison, if anybody sought a route simply leading, say from Kent to Westminster at that time, then Shooter's Hill lies near at hand and the plateau of Blackheath. It would hardly be necessary to trudge through the swampy ground right next to the water. Those who constructed those tracks must surely have had good reason to stay that close to the river.

One possibility is that the trackways led to platforms or hides, where men could lie in wait for waterfowl like geese and ducks. At the site in Uxbridge where the sedge marsh was burned, the bones of such birds dating from this period have indeed been found, which may be a clue as to what it was which attracted people to the water's edge in this way, to such an extent that they built permanent routes there. What is remarkable is the number of such trackways which have been found and the fact that whenever peat in the London area is delved into deeply enough, another of these things seems to turn up. Then too, there is the effect that such structures might have exercised upon the surrounding land.

Illustration 10 shows a sign on a footpath which crosses a marshy area in a great forest. Alongside this track is a deep bog, thousands of years old. This is like a living time capsule, for plants such as the carnivorous sundew grow here, as do water horsetails. The bog is also home to five different species of sphagnum moss. To one side, the land falls away sharply and the footpath follows the edge of an escarpment as it heads north. This is a part of Epping Forest which lays between the towns of Loughton and Epping, both of which have stations on the Central Line of the London Tube. The woodland here though looks positively primeval, and it is slightly uncanny to realize that you are walking along a track which was first laid down around 4,350 years ago. How are we able to be so sure about this date? The answer is simple.

This part of the forest has a number of springs and pools, making the ground soft and marshy. The footpath though has acted as a bank or dam, to prevent the springs to the north from draining into the lower ground. As a result of this, the bog has formed. Because this bog is such an unusual feature of the forest, it was investigated in the 1970s with a view to determining how old it was and how it had been formed. The answer was intriguing. A sample was taken of the bog, a core which reached to the very bottom, and the lowest part was carbon-dated to 4,340 years ago. This was at the end of the Neolithic. The implication was clear. The bog had been created by the building of the path which is now called Lodge

Road. The embankment which runs along the edge of the escarpment to form a way through the marshy ground, had the effect of preventing water draining from part of the forest. It was this which caused the bog to form.

That we can still walk along a trackway which was established over 4,000 years ago, is a strange thought. This is not though the only remaining trace of the network of tracks and roads which used to cover London during the Neolithic and Bronze Ages. On the fringes of the capital, in boroughs such as Redbridge and Havering, are patches of countryside and country parks such as Hainault Forest. Through these places are paths which are described as 'green lanes'. These are often all that remains of busy routes along which people walked, rode or drove herds of cattle and flocks of sheep. Sometimes, these paths are designated as bridleways, and some are called 'long greens'. In London itself, there are roads which are now called Green Lane, which often run straight as a Roman road from one point to another. The road called Green Lanes in North London, for instance, stretches north from Newington Green in Hackney, for six miles, all the way to Winchmore Hill. These roads too are relics of the distant past, places where we can faintly discern the pattern of prehistoric London. The more closely one examines the street map of London, the more one finds such old routes, which still follow the same line that they did before the Romans came to Britain.

The occasional inadvertent creation of a bog by building a trackway was one effect which the Neolithic people wrought upon the landscape. Another was the clearing of forests and all that resulted from this activity. These effects are, as you might say, merely by-products of the way of life of the people living in Britain at that time. They changed the landscape in other ways though, through the deliberate excavation and building of monuments to the dead and places to worship, and offer tribute to, their gods. Often, these two aims were combined, so that a sacred space ended up being used at one time for burying corpses and at others from presenting gifts to the gods. This led, over a long period of time, to the creation of what is sometimes known as the 'ritual landscape', a term that requires a little explanation.

In modern London, and indeed across the whole of Britain today, a sharp distinction is made between the secular and religious, and also between the world of the living and the realm of the dead. Often, these two concepts are melded together, so that that churches are combined with graveyards and the entire complex is separated from the rest of society by a physical barrier, typically a wall. Religion and death are thus kept apart from the world of the living, who wish to live their lives without being constantly reminded of either concept. So common is this arrangement that we hardly notice it at all. It is just how things are done. There is the everyday world of houses and shops, car parks and streets, and then there are little patches where the needs of prayer and the interment of the dead are attended to. We have no objection to statues or monuments in the street, dedicated to famous men and women, but we would feel uneasy if we knew that their physical remains were to be found within those structures, by the side of a public thoroughfare. In the same way, public exhibitions of religious devotion are generally felt to be inappropriate and embarrassing. There is a proper place for prayer and the worship of the Deity, and it is certainly not the middle of a street or town square. It was not always so.

So ingrained is our perception of the fitness of having a different zone of a city or town for religious functions or the burial of the dead, that even archaeologists are apt to impose this perspective on their discoveries of the past. When looking at the various prehistoric structures such as Stonehenge, Avebury and Silbury Hill, together with the enormous number of burial mounds scattered around that part of the county of Wiltshire, the expression 'ritual landscape' was coined. It was meant to signify that here was a large tract of land which was devoted to religion and the needs of the dead. It was assumed that such an area would be quite separate from those places where the people who built all those monuments actually *lived*. It is only in recent years, as evidence mounted and old ideas were questioned, that it has become obvious that this idea is false.

In two of the oldest human settlements that have been examined in recent year, Catal Huyuk in Turkey and Lepenski Vir in the Balkans, there did not seem to be any taboos around dead bodies, nor any separation between religious observance and everyday life. Both towns date from 5000 to 6000 BC. In Catal Huyuk, each house was found to have five or six skeletons buried beneath the floor. It seems that the practice had been to inter dead relatives beneath the domestic spaces of the living, a custom which most of us would regard as quite unacceptable these days. At Jericho in Israel, which dates from a thousand years earlier, human skulls were found which had been covered with clay and painted to resemble living heads. These were assumed to be ways of preserving the dead of the community, so that they could be kept around the home. In Lepinski Vir, every excavated home contained an altar, and images of fish gods were all over the place. For these people, religion was not divorced from day-to-day life, but was rather part and parcel of it.

Readers may wonder how all this relates to prehistoric London. The answer is that the area which became London was almost certainly a special kind of ritual landscape. The signs of this are all around, if only we know where to look. Take, for instance, the number of barrows or burial mounds which are scattered around the capital. Sailsbury Plain is of course famous for the tumuli which cover the area and form part of the ritual landscape. Everywhere one looks, there seem to be groups of hillocks and mounds which were constructed in the later Neolithic and early Bronze Age to act as repositories of, and memorials to, the dead. It is likely that the average Londoner will be quite unaware that his own city has plenty of such barrows, in all kinds of unexpected places. Illustration 11 shows a field of round barrows in central London, with the ultra-modern background of the towering skyscrapers of Docklands. The contrast between the ancient burial ground and the gleaming buildings could hardly be starker.

Erecting monuments was something which had been done before the arrival of the farmers, whose origins lay in Anatolia, but it was they who set out to make their mark on the land visually in a big way. The principal way in which they did this was by building highly visible tombs for their dead. These were what are known as long barrows and they were mounds of earth, and sometimes stone, which were built in rectangular shapes, probably to reflect the form of their own homes. The houses which have been excavated from this time, both in Britain and mainland Europe consist of long, rectangular buildings.

Only one long barrow still remains in London and it is to be found in Richmond Park. Later barrows, from the Bronze Age, are round and there are a number are scattered around the capital, but Richmond Park is the only surviving long barrow. It may be seen in Illustration 1, and it is in a pretty sad state. This is because a footpath cuts across it and has eroded the structure, until it is barely possible to make out the original form. It is today roughly oval, although it is likely that when first erected it was the same rectangular shape as the homes of those who built it. This long barrow is situated on the edge of an escarpment which sweeps down to the Thames. Placing the mound here would ensure that it was visible for miles around. It is about 150ft long and 65ft wide. Although the weather has worn away much of it over the last 6,000 years or so, it is still 10ft high. A visit to Richmond Park to see this barrow is well worth the effort, as it is the one of the few surviving fragments of the Neolithic ritual landscape around the Thames.

Because of all the building which has taken place in and around London over the last few centuries, it is no longer possible to see at a glance just how impressive such things as barrows would have been when first they began to appear. Richmond Park is on a very high bit of ground and the barrow could, when built, be seen for miles. We know this, for from the top of the barrow, it is possible to see the Surrey Hills. There is another barrow near to the long barrow at which we have been looking. This one is a round barrow and was built later than the long barrow. It is known today as Henry VIII's

Mound. It is called this due to an old legend, which holds that Henry VIII stood here on 19 May 1536, waiting to see a rocket fired from the Tower of London which would inform him that his wife, Anne Boleyn, had been executed and so he was free to marry Jane Seymour. The view from the top of this barrow is spectacular, so impressive in fact, that it is protected by law. Anybody standing on the barrow has a clear view, straight to central London, where the dome of St Paul's Cathedral may clearly be seen, even though it is 10 miles away. The view in the other direction is almost as extensive. These barrows were meant to be seen from far and wide.

The long barrow at Richmond would have been silhouetted against the sky when viewed from the Thames. It sits on what is technically known as the 'false horizon'; that part of a hill or escarpment which is as far as may be seen from a lower level. This arrangement was a common one with the builders of such tombs, not only in the Neolithic, but also in the Bronze Age and even later. Several examples are still to be found in London, two of which are actually in the heart of the city and will be examined in the next chapter. We are, however, not finished yet with what the long barrow in Richmond Park may be able to tell us about the way of life in London 5,000 years ago.

There are two chief differences between the barrows erected in the Neolithic and those of the Bronze Age. One of these is the shape and the other is that while the long barrows which have been investigated invariably contain the remains of more than one person, the round barrows only hold the skeleton or ashes of a single individual. Some bold conclusions have been drawn about this, such as that this change indicates that the

Neolithic people were more egalitarian and had no important leaders; in fact, that they were a more democratic society. It is suggested that the individual people buried in each round barrow, on the other hand, were members of some ruling elite and that this is why they were singled out for special treatment after death. As has been observed, trying to work out the mental processes of those who lived so long ago is a tricky and uncertain enterprise.

One idea about the barrows is that when built, they were intended simply to be houses for the dead. They were the same size as the houses in which people lived and were often provided with food, weapons and household goods which they might need in their new life. In such a case, what could be more natural than to make the mounds roughly the same size and shape as the houses of the living? Taking in account the effects of erosion over the passage of several thousand years, with wind and rain blurring the outline and erasing any sharp corners, it is altogether possible that the long barrows were originally rectangular, representing the long houses in which the farmers lived. In the same way, the round barrows *could* be said to be similar in a way to the roundhouses of Bronze Age Britain. A variation of this idea is that not only were the barrows built to *look* like the homes of the time, but were actually built on top of the actual houses in which had lived those who would be buried in the barrow. The size of the barrows fits in well enough with this idea. The long barrow in Richmond is almost 150ft long, quite of the right size to have been placed right over the remains of an actual long house. The same applies for round barrows. Illustration 2 shows a Bronze Age barrow on Plumstead Common in south

London. It is certainly large enough to fit the footprint of a roundhouse from that time. Unfortunately, neither of these theories is ever likely to be proved conclusively, intriguing though they may be.

Monuments to the dead were just one of the ways in which the farmers of the Neolithic sought to make their mark upon the land. There were other, more dramatic, means of doing so, once the forests had by been pushed back from the river by the establishment of fields. As the land became more open in aspect, it was used almost as a blank canvas, upon which the religious or spiritual visions of those living thereabouts were to be etched. The ritual landscape was about to come into being. If the size, shape and significance of the barrows is perplexing, it is nothing compared to some of the vast engineering projects undertaken near modern London, about whose purpose we have absolutely no idea whatsoever. At least we know that the barrows contained the remains of dead people, but a huge structure which lies partly buried beneath Terminal 5 of Heathrow Airport is an utter mystery.

When Terminal 5 was being built at Heathrow, archaeologists made the most of the opportunity to examine every square inch of the area which was soon to be covered with concrete. They found two ditches, running dead straight across the landscape, and at once assumed that this must be the remnants of a Roman road. The ditches were 22 yards apart and the earth which had been dug out from them was piled up between the two ditches to form a raised path. Who else would have been responsible for such a fine piece of surveying and construction work, if not the Romans? Two difficulties swiftly emerged with this interpretation of what was found. The first was that this supposed road didn't actually *lead* anywhere. It simply stretched for a little over two miles and then came to an abrupt halt. It also stopped at one bank of the River Colne and continued on the other side, although there was no trace of any bridge. Closer analysis showed that this odd feature had been laid out almost 6,000 years ago, long before the Romans arrived in Britain.

The technical name for a construction like the one found at Heathrow is a cursus. There are quite few scattered across the country, including one on Salisbury Plain, near Stonehenge. The name was coined by an eighteenth-century antiquarian, who thought that they resembled the tracks used in Roman times for chariot races, which were known as circuses. The one at Heathrow is called the Stanwell Cursus and it is a particularly long example. Every conceivable explanation has been advanced for the purpose of cursuses. These range from something to do with astronomical alignments to ancestor worship and ritual parades.

All we can say with assurance about cursuses is that they were not roads or tracks in the usual way that we think of such things. We know this because they have well-defined ends and lead nowhere in particular. A track leading from one settlement to another just a couple of miles away would in any case hardly necessitate the digging of deep ditches and building of a raised bank in the middle. The amount of work needed for such things must have been very great, and remember that these people were essentially subsistence farmers, who had to labour intensively just to produce the food necessary for their sustenance. Whatever a cursus was for, it must have been both very important and also had nothing to do with simply getting from A to B. The truth is, nobody has the remotest idea what they were used for. Some writers have advanced the idea that they were supposed to be some kind of route for ghosts to travel along; highways for the exclusive use of the spirits of the dead. This is an intriguing suggestion, but we are never likely to be sure at this late date what the purpose really was of such a structure. The same goes for what are known as causewayed enclosures, a number of which have also been found in and around London and which also date from the Neolithic.

At Staines, a few miles from the cursus at Heathrow Airport, is a Neolithic site consisting of two concentric circles of ditches, which enclose an area of over five acres. The ditches are interrupted at points, which provide entrances to the circular space within. These miniature causeways across the ditches are what led to such places being called 'causewayed enclosures'.

It must be said at once that, just as is the case with cursuses, nobody really knows why the causewayed enclosures were built. They were clearly a communal effort and a lot of work must have gone into planning and constructing them. The one at Staines has a diameter of around 500ft. They are clearly not meant as defensive fortifications, for why would you need half a dozen or more entrances? Evidence of both feasting and the burial of bodies has been found at causewayed enclosures and the current thinking is that they may perhaps be something like marketplaces or even the prehistoric equivalent of a town square; a place where people gathered to socialize and get together to exchange news, while at the same time enjoying a bite to eat. They may also have been somewhere that people from nearby settlements came to celebrate religious ceremonies, of course, but the evidence for any of these theories is either sparse or altogether lacking. One idea for the possible purpose of causewayed enclosures is macabre in the extreme.

The bones that are found in Neolithic long barrows seemingly had the flesh removed from them before they were placed in the tombs. Some of the long barrows are hollow, like houses, with shelves for the storage of disarticulated skeletons. Bones in them sometimes show signs of having been gnawed by animals, presumably when they were 'fresh', as one might say. This suggests that the corpses were exposed somewhere, and predators were allowed to strip away the flesh, before they were considered ready for burial or storage. This method of what is known technically as excarnation is still used today in India by the Parsees. These are members of the Zoroastrian religion who place corpses in specially constructed buildings, which are open to the sky at the top. These are known as Towers of Silence. Vultures and other birds come down and feed on the flesh and in the course of time, only the sun-bleached bones remain. It is thought by some archaeologists that the causewayed enclosures served a similar purpose. We know though that they were definitely used for drinking and eating, for the remains of such feasts have been found buried, along with human bones.

The strange possibility is raised that both the excarnation of human bodies and also the sharing of communal meals both took place in causewayed enclosures. Visitors might have come here, bringing with them the Neolithic equivalent of a picnic, and then sat down to eat and drink next to decaying corpses. Although such a scenario violates all our modern notions of what is fitting and acceptable behaviour, we have not the faintest idea of how the people in Britain 5,000 years ago would have felt about such an arrangement. As L.P. Hartley famously observed, 'The past is another country, they do things differently there'!

Most people have heard of Shepperton only in connection with the film studios found there, but it is almost certain that nobody reading this will ever have heard of Shepperton Henge. We are all of us familiar with Stonehenge, but Shepperton Henge? Before going any further, it might be a good idea to explain just what a henge is and why they are perhaps more common than one might think.

Henges are earthworks which were produced in Neolithic Britain. They are no more than round, vaguely circular, ditches, with the earth piled up into banks facing outward. There is no evidence of people living inside henges although sometimes there was what looks like ritual activity and some of them contained rings of standing stones or upright wooden posts. Others have avenues leading from them, which were also lined with wooden posts. That was the case at Shepperton Henge.

Shepperton is a village which lies on the north bank of the Thames, a few miles south of Heathrow Airport. It forms a triangle, when looked at in the context of the Stanwell Cursus and the causewayed camp at Staines, indicating that this was perhaps all part of a ritual landscape, centred around the Thames. The henge at Shepperton was probably an integral part of this arrangement. It consists of a circular ditch, the earth from which was piled up at the edge of the ditch. It was dug roughly 5,500 years ago. We have no idea at all why this spot was chosen and nor do we know what the actual purpose of the henge was. Two bodies were buried here, one of them a woman who, from analysis of her teeth, seemed to have grown up in an area where there were deposits of lead; the Mendips have been suggested as one possible childhood home, as has Derbyshire. Judging from the pottery found here, the henge was a place where feasting took place. We know too that this site was in use for a thousand years or more, for a hearth was uncovered and the ashes dated to about that length of time after the life of the woman whose skeleton was found there.

In 1963, a circular ditch dating to around 3000 BC was found in Rainham, now in in the London Borough of Havering. It was 50ft in diameter and a pit in the middle contained flints and fragments of pottery, but what purpose it might originally have served, it is impossible to say.

We have seen how ritual landscapes became a feature of Britain during the Neolithic era in various parts of the country, including the area around the Thames. The building of, and continuing work carried out upon, such things as barrows, henges and cursuses had implications which were not limited to the spiritual or religious. The practical effects of such enterprises were far-reaching in other ways and may be seen today, not least in London itself. Every time we travel along some of the major roads in and around the capital, we are following the same routes which were used 5,000 years ago to transport material across the country. People gathered together at important parts of London's ritual landscape and they used well-established tracks to get to this part of the Thames Valley.

It used to be thought that the Roman roads which have left their mark on the topography of Britain were a free creation of the occupiers; that they arrived and decided that it would be a good idea to have a straight road running from this place to that and then went about building it from scratch. This is not at all how the process really worked. There were already tracks leading to London, which were upgraded and then properly maintained by the Roman army. When they arrived, these were dirt tracks or drovers' roads, handy for driving herds of sheep from one place to another or to indicate to travellers which way they should be heading. These routes were established in the Neolithic, and we can still trace them today.

The people of the Mesolithic had no use for permanent tracks. They roamed the country, hunting animals and seeking berries, mushrooms, leaves and roots with which they could supplement their diet. Sticking to a fixed path when travelling would have been a very strange concept for them. Things changed of course when the farmers began crossing the Channel, 6,000 years ago or so. These were people who put down roots. They also wanted to spread out through Britain, looking for the best places to live and start planting crops. It was at this time that the part of the country we now call London became very important, for reasons which few of us would think of today.

Looking at a map of Britain and tracing the line of the Thames from Gloucestershire, where it begins, to the estuary which lies between Essex and Kent, it will be seen that the area south of this line is a very small portion of Britain; a thin slice, in fact. Assuming that those arriving from mainland Europe at the beginning of the Neolithic period in Britain crossed the English Channel at its narrowest point, surely a logical deduction, then this would mean that they landed somewhere near what is today Dover. Once they began making their way inland, the River Thames would be on their right hand, cutting them off from almost the whole of the new country. This might not matter for a generation or two, because of course there would be plenty of room in Kent and Sussex, but when the settlers wished to expand into the rest of Britain, they could only do so by heading north, at which point they would find their way blocked by the Thames. Of course, if they reached the Thames in Kent, then it would be far too wide to cross without building boats and so it would be natural to work their way west along the river, as it became narrower, until they found a spot where it could be forded.

It is almost certain that 6,000 years ago, there was a ford at that point where the River Effra enters the Thames from the south and the Tyburn does the same from the opposite bank. This is also where there is a sharp bend in the river and it was probably the tidal limit of the Thames at that time. This is the first point, when moving west from the Thames estuary, that it was possible to ford the river, simply to walk across it to the north bank. It is where Westminster is today. In fact, the river could still be forded here in modern times. Well, almost modern times. A somewhat eccentric British peer, Lord Noel-Buxton, was writing a book about ancient British history in the years following the end of the Second World War. After proving that at low tide it was possible to ford the River Humber, which separates Lincolnshire and Yorkshire, he decided to prove his theory that a there had indeed been a ford at Westminster and that it still existed. In March 1952, Noel-Buxton invited journalists to witness his fording the Thames at Westminster Bridge. He undertook the crossing at low tide and apart for a short period in the middle of the river, when his head disappeared beneath the surface, the crossing was a success.

Returning now to the prehistoric world, having found that this was the first crossing point where it was possible to wade across the Thames, it would have been natural for this spot to become of some importance and for tracks to lead to it. And in fact this is where the route known later as Watling Street crossed from south to north. It would have run west from Dover to the ford across the Thames and then from there it headed north into the rest of Britain. Later, the Romans built the first bridge over the Thames and Watling Street ended in the south at Southwark instead.

The ford at Westminster was probably of great significance to those living in Britain during the Neolithic for reasons other than the purely practical. In the last chapter we discussed the fact that this part of the river was a liminal zone, an in-between spot in several different ways. Apart from the general way in which rivers, lakes and pools of water were probably viewed as being portals to the world of the dead and land of the gods, Westminster had other characteristics, such as being the dividing point between fresh and brackish water and also the place where other rivers joined the Thames. Coming along the Thames from the east, this was not only the first point at which it was possible to wade across the river, it was the point at which the water became fresh and fit to drink. For these, and possibly other, reasons, this spot became the focus of veneration from at least the Mesolithic. It was almost certainly for this reason the posts at which we have looked were erected here, rather than anywhere else along the banks of the Thames. It became a place where sacrifices were made, of material objects which were cast into the water.

Axe heads made of jade have been found in the Thames. The material from which these has been crafted comes from Italy. Whether these axes were made there, or the raw material brought to Britain and the work carried out here, we have no way of knowing. A number of such jade axe heads have been found in this country and they date from the early years of the Neolithic. They have been found in rivers and bogs, where they were almost certainly deposited deliberately. One was found in the Thames. The sheer amount of work entailed in producing such an item is staggering. To bring the surface to such a state of smoothness, it has been estimated that around 100 hours of polishing would have been required. Of course, stone axes were being produced in huge numbers at this time, but there was no earthly reason why they would be polished in this way. The jade axe found in the Thames was never meant to be used in chopping down a tree, for which purpose it is, in any case, too thin. It is purely ornamental, that is to say made to be admired.

When we consider the enormous amount of work which went into manufacturing such things as jade axes, it is unlikely that the owner of such a prestigious article would be so careless as to lose it in a river. These things, including the one fished out of the Thames at Mortlake, were placed in the Thames in the same way that the Mesolithic hunters had been sacrificing their hand axes. The jade axes which have been found in the Thames and other rivers date back to the early days of farming in Britain, about 4000 BC. Such depositions were already an established custom at that time and would continue for at least the next 5,000 years. When the new inhabitants to live in the area around the Thames arrived in around 2300 BC, they simply continued many of the practices which they found, including the respect which the area in and around the ford at Westminster was accorded.

Chapter 5

The Bronze Age

For thousands of years, the Neolithic farmers who took over the Thames Valley from the hunter-gatherers who had previously occupied the area tilled the earth, cleared the forests and built the enigmatic monuments we now call the cursuses and causewayed enclosures. They must have felt secure in their hold on the territory, because they had managed to conquer the wildwood and impose their will upon the very land, creating the ritual landscape around them. Perhaps it seemed to them that nothing would ever change the way of life which they led and that any changes, if and when they did occur, would always be gradual and take place over the course of many generations. The Neolithic Age in Britain lasted roughly as long as the period of time between Julius Caesar's first landing in 55 BC and the present day. And then, everything *did* change, without warning and with dizzying rapidity. Even before that though, those farming the land near the Thames were, like everybody else in Neolithic Europe, in difficulty.

A study conducted at the University of Gothenburg in 2018 revealed that the teeth of those Neolithic people being examined were harbouring plague bacteria. This disease was an ancestor of the Black Death which devastated medieval Europe. It was perhaps hardly surprising, because the lifestyle in the Neolithic was ideally suited to spread disease. The population was growing, which meant that people were huddled together in larger settlements. The typical houses in which they lived were divided into two sections. One was the living area for people and the other was where the livestock was kept. It was, for the average family, like living in a barn. We have in recent years seen how diseases can jump from some animal species and mutate to infect humans, as is supposed to have happened with Covid-19. Here were perfect conditions for such a thing to occur.

All the indications are that by about 4,500 years ago, the farmers of Britain and mainland Europe were on the decline. They were decimated by illness and their general health was not very good. The larger settlements had been abandoned, sometimes deliberately burned down. This was a culture which had passed its peak and had nowhere to go. We saw in the last chapter that farmers of Europe at that time sometimes did very well, and their communities grew large, but that following blights on their crops or a run of poor summers, then the opposite might happen and numbers would fall. They were hanging on and surviving, but not, looked at over a time scale of centuries, really progressing.

Five or six thousand years ago, in what is now Ukraine and Western Russia, a confederation of tribes lived whose culture is known as the Yamnaya; a name derived from the burial mounds which they constructed for their dead. These people were pastoralists, who kept herds of cattle and flocks of sheep and goats. Pastoralism is a branch of agriculture, know sometimes as animal husbandry. Those who practise this way of life are usually nomadic, moving from place to place so that there is sufficient space for their animals to graze. Pastoralism is on the decline in the modern world, for it requires large, open spaces and a disregard often for frontiers and national borders. The Bedouin of the Sinai desert are nomadic pastoralists of this kind, moving from place to place with their camels and goats, in search of suitable spots to graze their herds.

The Yamnaya were also workers in copper and owned both domesticated horses and wheeled carts, these probably being drawn by oxen rather than horses. They spoke Proto Indo-European, the language which later split into almost all the European and Indian languages which we know today; from English to Punjabi, and Swedish to Urdu. It is thought that they lived in tents or temporary shelters such as huts, never remaining long in any one location. Despite this, the various clans and tribes were not wholly disconnected and independent entities. There was much communication between the groups, and the common language meant that they understood each other.

Around 2500 BC, the Yamnaya began to scatter to the four corners of the earth, for reasons which we are only able to guess at. It may simply have been that the steppe was becoming too crowded or perhaps a harsh season had dried up the grass and led to an inability to stay in their homeland. Or it could be that restlessness set in and the tribes began to yearn for something new. Some groups moved east and colonized part of China, others moved south and then east. These people found their way into what is now Turkey and Iran and ultimately India. And of course, a large body of the Yamnaya set out west, their ox-drawn carts probably resembling nothing so much as a wagon train in nineteenth-century America, as emigrants went in search of new lands.

The invasion and colonization of Europe by the Yamnaya and their descendants has been described by some writers as a violent tide, sweeping across the continent. A recent article even went so far as to talk of 'genocide'. Of course, this was not a horde of savage warriors, behaving like the armies of Genghis Khan, but an altogether slower conquest; one which took centuries to accomplish. It was perhaps achieved partly by force of arms, but also, and perhaps more importantly, by the possession of superior technology, coupled with a way of life which promised more benefits than that which was currently being pursued. The superior advantages of copper and bronze tools and the use of wheels was plain and although some reactionaries might have preferred to stick to the old methods and harvest crops with sickles made of flint, this way of life soon became obsolete.

This is not to say that there were not massacres and rape, as the farming communities found their lands being colonized. It would have been surprising had there not been some resistance to the newcomers. There were clashes and raids, but who precipitated them, the invaders or those whose land they were usurping, it is impossible now to say. What *can* be said with assurance is that the farmers were replaced and their genetic inheritance obliterated. It must be borne in mind that the Yamnaya were taller, stronger and more healthy than the farmers they encountered. Their diet essentially consisted of meat and milk, combined with what they could forage as they travelled, in the way of roots, fruit, nuts and edible leaves. These were a tough and healthy breed of people.

Eventually, around 2400 BC, the great-great-grandchildren of the Yamnaya began to arrive in Britain and within a few centuries had replaced the Neolithic farmers there almost entirely. In the Thames Valley, especially around London, they

Above: 1. The Neolithic burial mound which stands on the edge of an escarpment in Richmond Park.

Below: 2. A so-called 'round barrow', a Bronze Age mound on Plumstead Common in south London.

3. A nodule of flint forming the fossil of a sea urchin, found in south London.

Left: 4. The ancient seabed of south London.

Below: 5. The fossilized remains of sea creatures which lived near London, 55 million years ago.

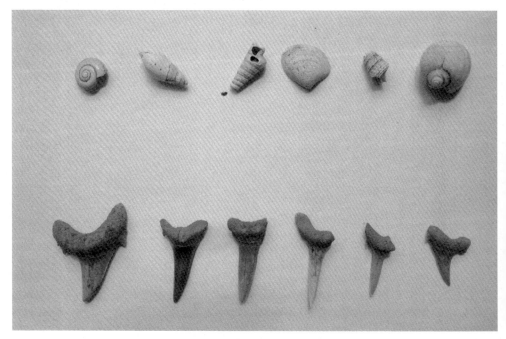

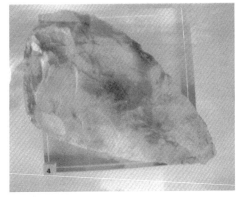

Above left: 6. A Palaeolithic hand axe.

Above right: 7. A sign forbidding people to cast money into a coffin.

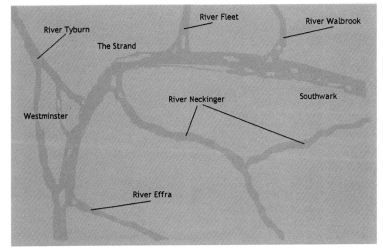

8. Rivers of central London, which now flow underground.

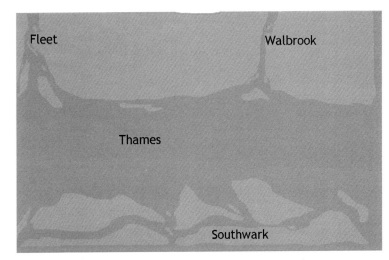

9. Prehistoric Southwark, a district of islands.

Above: 10. A Neolithic track through a dangerous bog near London.

Below: 11. A barrow field near London's Docklands.

Above: 12. The so-called 'Waterloo Helmet', over 2,000 years old.

Right: 13. A magnificent bronze shield, recovered from the Thames.

Below: 14. The Bell Barrow at Hampstead, in central London.

Above: 15. The Shrewsbury tumulus.

Below: 16. The temple in Greenwich Park.

Right: 17. The Dagenham Idol.

Below: 18. The way up to the hill fort of Charlton Camp.

Above: 19. The view across London from the vicinity of Loughton Camp.

Below: 20. Amesbury Banks, where Boudicca's last stand reputedly took place.

found a ritual landscape which they soon began to remodel after their own fashion. These immigrants were not barbarians and rather than destroy the existing monuments and religious customs, they adopted them and altered them so that they would be more in keeping with their own belief system. It was probably these newcomers who also gave names to this part of Britain which are still in use today, calling the river the Thames and that section which lay roughly between Vauxhall and the Isle of Dogs, they named London.

Not only did the Yamnaya bring horses, wheels and metal-working into Europe, they also brought a new language, new religious beliefs and social arrangements. These things were to effect just as great a change on Britain as the ability to forge weapons of bronze or ride on horseback. It was the ideas of those who were to settle in the Thames Valley which created most of the remaining physical signs of the distant past which remain today, rather than any advance in agriculture or the ability to wage war with stronger weapons.

Just as close examination of the ancient languages of Greece, Rome and India tell us that a common language was once spoken by the ancestors of the Hindus, Greeks, Italians and British, so can looking at their history and legends indicate something of the original beliefs of those from whom those nations and cultures sprang. In India, thousands of years ago, just as in Athens, Rome and Celtic Britain, the population was divided into three broad categories. In India, this division was codified into sacred scripture and still remains of great importance to this day. We see the same thing in the writings of the Roman Empire and traces of it are discernible too in old Irish legends. This tripartite arrangement of society meant that almost everybody belonged to one of three social classes; namely farmers, warriors or priests. The category of priests was sometimes interchangeable with that of royalty.

The division of society into three categories or castes was not the only change which the descendants of the Yamnaya introduced to Britain. There was another, which was to be more profound and which we still observe to this day. It was caused by the technology upon which these newcomers depended. The reliance upon metal alloys introduced a new imperative to ancient Britain, the need to trade in order to survive.

During the Neolithic, farmers could survive pretty much on what they produced. There was no particular need to establish contact with people hundreds of miles away. That is not to say of course that no trade took place. What exchanges and bartering did occur though was often about what people *wanted*, rather than what they *needed*. There was for example an 'axe factory' at Langdale in the Lake District. Stone axes from this area have been found in East Anglia and as far away as France. The stone found at Langdale was very beautiful when polished and it is likely that the axes made from it were valued as much for their aesthetic appeal as for being of practical use. There was plenty of flint to be found in East Anglia for the manufacture of axes and so it was not strictly necessary for a trade route to develop in this way. The case was quite different when the use of bronze became widespread.

In the London area, there is no shortage of flint and indeed there are Mesolithic sites at Hampstead Heath and in Epping Forest where flint tools were made. Flint is found in many places in and around London, especially those which are on high ground and also sandy or chalky. This is not at all the case with copper and tin, the constituents of bronze. The nearest source of tin to London is in the West Country and copper is to be found in Wales. This in turn meant that if those arriving in Britain wished to maintain their modern lifestyle, using metal instead of stone for their weapons and tools, then it would be necessary to establish regular trade routes and to regulate the economy of their settlements. This was vital, for if the settlers near the Thames were unable to get hold of copper and tin, then they would be forced to decline culturally, to revert to the use of stone and follow a more primitive lifestyle. Since there was little appetite for such a course of action, the newcomers had no option but to modernize Britain in other ways, by setting up new ways of living which would, from the beginning, rely upon others who lived hundreds of miles away. The effect of this was both social and psychological, because it meant that no longer would a family in the Thames Valley just live by themselves on their own resources. They were now compelled to look outwards and to deal with others. This requirement automatically had the effect of creating a more complex society, one in which some men pursed trades such as smiths and potters, while others engaged in transporting goods from place to place across the country. Then too, miners would also be necessary, to dig out the copper and tin. It meant that men would from then on be separated into classes or professions. Some would till the earth and raise crops, while others would work in copper mines. Some men became smiths, which was from the beginning a highly respected occupation. Then too, there would be traders, those who arranged to transport and sell copper mined in Wales to those near London who needed the metal.

There can be no doubt that all this had such a lasting effect upon the landscape, that even today we can see traces of the changes in London, a point to which we shall return shortly. One change which arrived with the Bronze Age was in the shape of the buildings in which people lived. The Neolithic homes were rectangular, but those of the new inhabitants were round. It is not inconceivable that these round huts were made in imitation of the tents in which the forefathers of the new Europeans had lived when they were nomads. It was remarked earlier that it may be the case that Neolithic barrows were shaped as they were because they represented the houses of the living, in which case it was reasonable to suppose that the barrows of those who introduced the roundhouses to Britain should themselves be round.

Still on the subject of shape, it is interesting to note that although during the Bronze Age in Britain, people lived in roundhouses, their temples were either rectangular or square. When they *were* round, then a rectangular enclosure surrounded them. For instance, the remains of a village were found at Heathrow, dating from a little later than the Bronze Age, and all the homes were round. There was however a temple there and this was rectangular in shape. For some reason, even a couple of thousand years after the end of the Neolithic period, this layout was felt to be suitable for religious buildings. The same design is seen in temples of this time all over Britain.

When Heathrow Airport was being built in 1944, a village was uncovered which dated from about 200 BC. There were eleven typical roundhouses of the time and also a rectangular structure which has been interpreted as a temple. Two thousand years after the descendants of the Yamnaya had arrived in that part of the Thames Valley and swept away the Neolithic society which they found there, sacred buildings were still being modelled on those in which the farmers of the Neolithic had lived. This too is very likely an instance of an old tradition being preserved when it came to matters of religion.

The part of the Thames which eventually became London was already important, long before the coming of these new settlers. The ford at Westminster and the road leading to it from Dover had already been in use for many centuries. There were also religious or ritual associations with this part of the river, indicated by not only the Mesolithic structure at Vauxhall, but also the sacrifices or deposits made in the water and in holes dug on the shore. Such important places were recognized and respected by the newcomers. Just as they continued to venerate the area of Sailsbury Plain where Stonehenge stands, and also continued to develop the monuments there, so too was London accepted as a special location. Once again, it is in the disposal of the dead that we are able to glean some understanding of the way that the land in and around what is now London was regarded at that time.

It is only relatively recently that we have been able to hazard a tentative guess about the population during the Bronze Age of that part of South East England which would one day become London. For many years, it was assumed that this was a sparsely settled region, consisting in the main of isolated farmsteads, with small hamlets to be found here and there. It now seems unlikely that this was the case and in fact the area was far more densely inhabited than we ever suspected. Such a conclusion entails extrapolating from meagre archaeological evidence, but if correct, gives us a startling new perspective on what the prehistoric landscape would have looked like before a city was built here. Imaginative reconstructions of what the Bronze Age and Iron Age were like in this country usually show a bare landscape. Even when a hill fort is depicted, full of roundhouses, there are seldom roads in the picture, connecting the place with anywhere else. Most often, the scene will be stretches of open country, suggesting that the land was pretty empty at that time and habitations few and far between. After all, if people lived in Britain and were largely self-sufficient through farming and hunting, there wouldn't be any *need* for roads, would there? We all know that it was not until the Romans turned up and began building their famously solid and workmanlike routes there were any proper roads in Britain. All the evidence we now have leads us to suppose that this view of the past is hopelessly inaccurate.

It is only relatively recently that we have begun to be so meticulous in London about preserving the heritage of the past. When a Tube station was being built near the Tower of London in 1882, the one we now know of as Tower Hill station, the builders encountered a serious obstacle, which was a long stretch of the Roman city wall, which lay below street level. So soundly constructed was it, that it soon became clear that men hacking away with pickaxes would take months to remove it. A simple expedient was found by means of a few kegs of gunpowder, which made short work of 2,000 years of the city's history. In much the same way, when digging through layers of peat in east London to lay foundations for some new building or other, a lot of old sticks were found, they were simply thrown into a refuse heap. Those old sticks though, which these days we treat with enormous care, might have told us a lot about London's past.

It was remarked above that the effect of the trade routes established in and around London during the Bronze Age are still visible. Once you know where to look, the signs are glaringly obvious. The London Boroughs of Havering, Newham, and Barking and Dagenham were marshy and often waterlogged during the Bronze Age. These days, with the Thames and the Roding confined behind concrete embankments, they are a good deal drier than they were thousands of years ago, when the land would be swamped for miles around whenever some heavy rain caused the level of the rivers to rise by a metre or two. It was of course for this reason that wooden trackways began to be constructed, the kind of thing at which we have already looked. What astonished some archaeologists though, was that these trackways seemed to be found everywhere that a deep hole was dug through peat and a proper examination conducted of what lay beneath the surface. It seemed that almost every time anybody looked into a hole excavated deeply enough in east London, that another trackway was uncovered.

In 1994, archaeologist Frank Meddens, from Newham's Passmore Edwards Museum, was interviewed by the *Independent* newspaper. He said, 'Every time we dig a hole anywhere in the southern parts of the boroughs of Havering, Barking and Newham we come across evidence of prehistoric trackways'. Meddens went on to explain that he estimated that such trackways, leading to the river, would have been encountered every third of a mile or so, suggesting strongly that far more people lived in the marshy area which now makes up the easternmost boroughs of London than had previously been thought. Most of the constructions, which sometimes led to wooden platforms, which might have been landing stages for boats, had been dated to the Bronze Age, although some were older.

As was remarked above, it is only in the last few decades that anybody has taken notice of such things. After all, when all is said and done, the remains being uncovered are not particularly impressive to the average person. They comprise soggy and blackened sticks and brushwood, the significance of which is not immediately apparent.

The idea of a network of footpaths, tracks and even roads crisscrossing London, thousands of years before the Romans, is an odd one and does not readily accord with our notions of the way that the country was at that time. Yet a moment's thought will soon tell us that people still needed to get about and move from place to place. It would have made no sense at all for each man to forge a new path every time he wished to pass through a forest or cross a marsh. Anybody who has gone for a walk through dense woodland will know how long it takes to move through a thickly wooded area where there are no paths at all. It is a time-consuming and tiring process, and it would have been in the interests of everybody if at least some rough paths could be established through wooded or waterlogged parts of the landscape. However sparsely scattered the population was at that time, it would have made sense for groups of people to band together in the common interest to agree to lay. and perhaps maintain, routes from one part of the Thames Valley to another.

Traces of the trackways and paths which once crisscrossed Greater London are still visible today, if one knows where to look. The streets of London are like a palimpsest, a manuscript which has been overwritten, but leaving traces of the previous text still faintly visible. Take the famous Roman road known as Watling Street, for instance. This was not designed and built from scratch by the Romans, but rather followed an existing British track. The northern branch of Watling Street, which has been a route towards North Wales for well over 2,000 years when the Romans arrived, may still be travelled today and indeed clearly identified on a modern London street map.

One thing which is very noticeable when looking at a map of London is that several main roads in and out of London travel in more or less straight lines, from the centre to the suburbs and beyond. One such route is Edgeware Road, which stretches north-west from Marble Arch, becoming after a few miles Maida Vale, and then Kilburn High Road. It continues up, past Brent Cross Shopping Centre. This is all part of Watling Street. If we take a ruler and then extend the line of this perfectly straight road south-east, towards the Thames, it reaches Westminster Bridge. This is a clear indication that this old track used to lead to the ford there, before the coming of the Romans.

The significance of this particular route during the Bronze Age should be immediately obvious. Watling Street, which was probably at that time a broad grassy track, leading north-west towards Wales, led to the main source of copper used in Britain during the Bronze Age. It went first to Verlamian, an oppidum or small town which later became a Roman city called Verulamium. We know this today as St Albans. From there, it headed to the modern village of Wroxeter. At that point, one track led north and the other west, leading to the Isle of

Anglesey. And it was there, at a site which we call the Great Orme now, that the main copper mine in the country at that time was found. Copper from there was transported across the whole of Britain, some of it even finding its way to Europe. The track or road between Anglesey and the ford across the Thames was probably the most important route in Britain during the centuries when bronze was the most important metal in use.

There are in London other routes of this kind, which even today can be traced on a map and show their ancient origins. Take Fenchurch Street in central London, for instance, which runs from the vicinity of the Monument and then becomes Whitechapel High Street. Its name then changes, and it is called Whitechapel Road and then Mile End Road. It mutates into Romford Road, Ilford High Road and various other names, as it heads north-east. This is the old Colchester Road and it runs in a more or less straight line to that town. Colchester was a Roman city and the road we have traced follows the Roman road, but before the Romans constructed both the city and the road, there was the oppidum of Camulodunon and a track ran from there to the ford across the Thames at Westminster. The more closely one examines the street map of London, the more one finds such old routes, which still follow the same line that they did before the Romans came to Britain.

London was then, over a thousand years before the Romans decided to establish a city here, an important place in Britain. Trade routes led here and those crossing the English Channel from the European mainland were obliged to come to this part of the Thames if they wished to cross the river and head further north. Boats would sail along the Rhine from central Europe and then travel up the Thames to the tidal head of the river at modern-day Westminster. This was, in secular terms, an important location. There was though another reason for coming to the area near the ford, other than for reasons of travel and trade. It was also the centre of religious devotion in Britain.

Much of our knowledge about prehistoric London comes from things which have been willingly cast into the Thames and its tributaries or thrown down wells or shafts dug into the earth nearby for that purpose. The only example in the world of a horned bronze helmet from the Iron Age may be seen in Illustration 12. It was pulled from the Thames near Waterloo Bridge in 1868 and is now in the British Museum. Such helmets are shown in carvings and other images from mainland Europe, but this is the only actual specimen ever found. It is made of very thin sheets of bronze and would have been quite useless for actually protecting anybody's head during a battle. It is purely decorative or ceremonial. The same is true of the shield shown in Illustration 13, which was found in the river at Battersea, 10 years before the helmet, and dates from roughly the same period. This too was beautifully made but far too fragile ever to have been used in combat. It was merely to be admired. How on earth then did such valuable pieces of gear come to be lost in the river, with nobody trying to retrieve it?

The general consensus among archaeologists is that these items, along with other shields, swords and all manner of things, were deliberately cast into the water as sacrifices to the gods. This makes sense, because there were lakes in Britain and mainland Europe which, when drained, were found to be full of all weapons, coins, jewellery, bridles and many other things which would have been worth a great deal at the time that they were thrown into the water. It is thought that special platforms were constructed, so that those wishing to sacrifice their goods in this way could be sure to do so in the deepest part of the river or lake. It is likely that just such a structure has been uncovered in the centre of London.

Near the Mesolithic posts which were found just by the MI6 building, remnants of another set of ancient wooden posts had already been found in 1993. These have been dated to 1500 BC, during the Bronze Age, and they consist of two rows of posts leading out into the river. At first, their purpose was obscure. Could they be part of the earliest bridge ever built across the Thames? This seemed unlikely, because the river was a lot wider at the time that that these posts were driven into the ground and it is likely that bridging such an expanse of water would have been an unnecessary enterprise, because there was a perfectly good ford at Westminster, just a short walk away. Another idea was that this might be the remains of a jetty, somewhere to tie up boats or unload cargo. Neither explanation is altogether convincing, and there is a third possibility.

At a place called Flag Fen in East Anglia, are the remains of a long causeway or bridge which 2,500 years ago, stretched for a kilometre across watery fenland. Thousands of wooden stakes were used to build it, and halfway across the water was a huge wooden platform. It was at first thought that this might have been a lake village, of the kind sometimes seen at this period in parts of Europe. Militating against such an hypothesis is the fact that in the years since it was discovered, not a single trace of any habitation has been found on or near the platform. It almost seems as though this was a bridge leading to a platform built for no particular reason. This too, goes to show the perils of examining the distant past and assuming that men and women at that time had a mindset even remotely like our own. The causeway and platform at Flag Fen would have been a simply astonishing project, involving an immense amount of work and yet there is nothing to indicate what this wooden platform could have been used for. There are, however, clues.

Many swords and daggers have been recovered at Flag Fen, along with jewellery and other valuable objects. Many of the swords had been symbolically destroyed, rendered unusable by being twisted or broken. It seems likely that this was a place where people came to sacrifice belongings which were precious to them. Francis Pryor, who excavated Flag Fen, has suggested that such sacrifices were carried out for religious reasons, but also as a way for wealthy and prominent people to demonstrate just how important and well-off they were, by throwing articles of great value into the water in this way. It might, in other words, have been a form of what is sometimes known as conspicuous consumption; a vulgar display to show how rich somebody is by throwing their money around publicly.

Flag Fen is not unique. Scattered across Europe and dating from the Bronze Age, are sites which were evidently constructed and used for the ritual deposition or sacrifice of objects which were of considerable value to those giving them up. The very name of the Celtic culture of the latter part of the Iron Age in Europe derives from just such a place.

On the north side of Lake Neuchâtel in Switzerland is the village of La Tène, after which an entire culture has been named. The reason for this was that during a drought in 1857 the level of the lake fell dramatically and revealed many swords and shield bosses, along with a great quantity of jewellery. There were also wooden posts, like those later found in London, which had, as we mentioned earlier, been considered as possibly forming a bridge. Those at La Tène formed part of a short pier, which led out towards the middle of the lake. A curious circumstance was that the swords recovered from this lake showed no sign of wear. They had seemingly been thrown into the water from the jetty or pier, brand-new; just as they had been made.

On the Isle of Anglesey, off the coast of Wales, is a lake called Llyn Cerrig Bach. Anglesey was of course the centre of Druid power in Britain and it seems that people from southern Britain made pilgrimages here to sacrifice at the lake. During the Second World War, an airfield was being built here, which necessitated clearing the area in and around the lake. An iron chain was found, which was used for hauling vehicles which had become stuck in the mud, by pulling them with a tractor. The chain was of a curious design though and when, eventually, archaeologists got wind of what was being found during the excavations at Llyn Cerrig Bach, they soon identified the chain as one used to link together slaves or prisoners. This was not the only interesting item dredged up at this location. Seven swords, six spearheads, parts of a cauldron and various other metal objects were recovered from the bog on the edge of the lake. Some were bronze and others made of iron and the weapons had been ritually damaged before being deposited. It was thought that this had been a religious site, where people came from miles away to make sacrifices to the gods.

It is entirely possible, likely even, that the part of the Thames where London is now was another such place, like Flag Fen, La Tène and Llyn Cerrig Bach, where votive offerings were made into the water. This would perfectly explain the great variety of valuable swords, helmets, shields and other articles which have over the years been dredged up from the river in and around London. The posts dating from the Bronze Age at Vauxhall might, by this reading of the situation, have formed a short pier, leading to a platform from which ritual depositions might have been made in the river. These would, presumably, have been made as part of some public ceremony. After all, there would be little point in hurling a hugely expensive bronze shield away, as though it were a piece of rubbish, unless lots of people could witness your extravagance! There are grounds for supposing that this was the true purpose of the structure, because when it was being examined by archaeologists, two bronze spearheads were found, driven deep into the mud in which the posts had been hammered. These spearheads had not simply been lost. Both were point down in the ground and had obviously been thrust in at the same time that the posts were being erected for the walkway out into the river. These were definitely sacrificial offerings of some kind.

The pier at Vauxhall, alongside the Mesolithic posts, would have been one part of the ritual landscape which surrounded this part of the Thames at that time. One would actually have to make a pilgrimage to the riverbank though in order to see them. The most significant and visually striking ritual structures though, were in a quite a different league. They could be seen for literally miles. It may surprise readers to learn that even today, there are Bronze Age mounds in London which can be seen from between 10 to 15 miles away.

In the last chapter we looked at a Neolithic barrow in Richmond; a burial mound designed to hold the remains of more than one person and possibly modelled on the plan of the houses of the living at that time. The men and women of the Bronze Age continued to model and adapt the landscape in a very noticeable fashion to commemorate their dead. In this way, they modified the existing ritual landscape of the London area until it bore a distinct similarity to that around Stonehenge. Because the traces of their activities in this field are the most noticeable remnants of their occupation, it is at these that we shall first look.

The shape of barrows changed at about the time that the new wave of settlers arrived in Britain, although cultural influences had already led to some alteration in the practices around burials in this country. The main difference was that whereas before the barrows had been rectangular or oval in shape, they were now round. A number of these round barrows are still to be seen in London.

The primary purpose of raising an imposing mound over the remains of a dead person is of course to commemorate him or her and to ensure that their memory lives on after death. It makes sense therefore that such monuments should be in prominent locations; places where people will see them from afar and perhaps pass by them frequently. Of course, we have followed a similar practice in modern times. One need only think of Nelson's Column to see an example of making a memorial to a dead person visible from a long way off. The same consideration applies to all those statues of Victorian soldiers and statesmen scattered around central London. These monuments are not hidden away in alley ways and obscure turnings, but positioned in main streets, so that every passer-by will notice them. This was precisely the principle adopted in Bronze Age Britain, and London has some splendid examples of barrows from this time which still have a commanding presence.

One way of drawing attention to a monument is to make sure that it is in a high place, where people from all around will be able to see it and there is certainly good evidence in London for this practice during the Bronze Age. The long barrow at which we looked in Richmond Park is a case in point, situated as it is on the edge of an escarpment, where anybody by the river below will be able to see it merely by looking up. Such monuments might be said to dominate a landscape. Not far from that barrow is a round barrow and this really is beautifully situated to be seen from almost anywhere in London. Today, this barrow is known as King Henry's Mound. The view from the top encompasses both St Paul's Cathedral, in the centre of London, and Windsor Castle in Berkshire. In fact, King Henry's Mound is a round barrow, which probably dates from between 2400 and 1500 BC. It would be hard to find a more visible landmark, which is visible for many miles to both east and west.

Placing barrows on the highest parts of hills which are visible from the ground below was a popular position for round barrows during the Bronze Age. It is in central London that the most perfectly preserved example of a Bronze Age barrow is to be found and it is also of a very unusual type. Quite how this burial mound escaped destruction and lingered on in the middle of London is an interesting point.

Hampstead Heath is a sprawling area of wild woodland and heath which has survived unchanged for centuries and has never been built on. It consists of some 800 acres of the highest land in London, with spectacular views from Epping Forest in the north to the Surrey hills in the south. It is known that Mesolithic hunters camped here and there is evidence too of Neolithic activity. None of this can be seen today and the only remnant of the prehistoric past is the barrow which stands over 300ft above sea level on a ridge of land forming part of Parliament Hill. This has been known for many years as Boadicea's Grave, although there is not the least reason to suppose that there is any connection with the Iceni queen. There is also an old legend which suggests that this is the last place in London where fairies were seen. Barrows of this kind were, in the past, often associated with the supernatural.

The Hampstead bell barrow, which may be seen in Illustration 14, sits at the top of a steep slope, with the ground falling away to the north and east, affording a spectacular perspective of north London and Essex. In the distance, about 15 miles away, can be seen Epping Forest. This would also be the case with the Shrewsbury Barrow on the side of Shooters Hill, in south London, if it were not for the houses which block the line of sight. Otherwise, it would be possible to see right the way across London to Essex from that point. We can be sure of this, because the whole of Shooters Hill is visible from a hill on the fringes of Epping Forest. Illustration 19 shows this view. These barrows were designed to sit on the false horizon when viewed from the ground below and also to be seen from miles around. There may of course have been another reason for placing the burial mounds on hills in this way, which is that height could, in itself, have been thought to be a desirable thing for religious activities and those involving the afterlife.

In the Old Testament, there are clues as to what kind of beliefs might have motivated the Bronze Age population of Britain. We have already mentioned one such common theme, which relates to sacred poles or pillars, but other religious practices might also shed light on what we see in prehistoric London. One of these is the reverence for what are referred to repeatedly 'high places'. In ancient Israel, the Canaanites went to the top of hills to be closer to their gods, presumably because the higher they climbed, the nearer they were to the sky, where some of their gods dwelled. This feeling, that the higher you climbed the nearer you might be to the abode of the gods, can be seen in other ancient cultures, besides that of the Israelites and Canaanites. The building of tall artificial structures such as the pyramids of Egypt, the towers of Mesopotamia and even the huge stone ritual structures of the Aztecs, are all probably connected with this idea. On Salisbury Plain in Britain stands Silbury Hill; an artificial mound which has roughly the same height and volume as the largest of the Egyptian pyramids. Like them, and other ziggurats and raised platforms, including those in central America, the purpose of such a construction was to reach as high into the sky as possible.

It is still possible to work out how the barrow on Parliament Hill was made. A circular ditch can still be made out, which is perhaps 150ft in diameter. This is what is known as a 'quarry ditch', from which earth was excavated and piled within the ring to form a platform. The actual barrow, which is 100ft wide, is set in the centre of the platform. It is 9ft high in the middle. The whole thing has a very distinctive shape, which is what led to such burial mounds being called bell barrows, of course.

Standing by this barrow impresses upon the visitor just how visible this spot would once have been. The whole of north London is laid out before us and the hills of Hertfordshire and Essex are clearly visible. Before building began, anybody on the plain below would have seen the outline of the barrow against the sky. This is indeed a 'high place', about as high as one can get in the centre of London.

There is some reason to think that Hampstead Heath and Parliament Hill were sites of religious significance for thousands of years and perhaps part of a particular ritual landscape. In 2017, an archaeological excavation at the top of Parliament Hill uncovered evidence of another Bronze Age feature and it appeared that fires had been lit here during that time. Then too, there is the curious earthwork known as the 'Saxon Ditch'. This ditch and bank runs for some distance across the heath. It is called the 'Saxon' Ditch, because it was first recorded in the tenth century, but there is no reason to suppose that that was when it was created. It is entirely possible that this too is a relic of a much earlier age.

There is another viewpoint in central London which was probably used for the raising of a burial mound and it is to be found south of Hampstead and right next to Regent's Park. This is Primrose Hill, which is, like Parliament Hill and Shooters Hill, something of a viewpoint across London. A southern ridge of Primrose Hill was known until the nineteenth century as Barrow Hill, due to burial mounds on it. It was razed over 150 years ago, in order to dig a reservoir.

South of the Thames, still in central London, is another barrow placed on a hill, so that it could be seen for miles. This one is situated on what is known as the 'false horizon', the brow of a hill viewed from below, and may be found in the most unexpected of spots; namely a heavily built-up area near Shooters Hill in South London. It is part of a chain of barrows which stretched along the side of the hill and also lined the route of Watling Street, which passed a few miles to the north.

Thousands of years before the Romans came to this part of Britain, an ancient track ran from Dover to London, where it was possible to ford the Thames and then continue to the other parts of the country. Today, Shooters Hill Road, the old Dover Road, runs over the crest of Shooters Hill and carries on west, along the high ground of Blackheath. This is very likely the same route along which Watling Street once ran.

On a low hill on Plumstead Common, not far from Woolwich, stands a Bronze Age bowl barrow, which may seen in Illustration 2. It is greatly eroded by the passage of time and now stands only 3 or 4ft high. When it was constructed, there would have been a ditch around this burial mound, which is perhaps 50ft across. This is the last surviving barrow from a group of seven which once stood here. There are records of these in the nineteenth century, but since then, the others have gradually been flattened, so that the common is a smooth area, suitable for playing ball games on. Watling Street would have passed close to these mounds during the Bronze Age and anybody heading inland from Dover would have seen them. Not only would travellers have been able to see these barrows, they would also have been afforded a clear view of another group, up on the hillside to their right as they made their way to the ford at Westminster.

Illustration 15 is of a most unusual archaeological site. We are most of us familiar with images of Salisbury Plain and other areas of open country, where round barrows jut up from the fields. Photographs of that kind are something we know, and the concept of the ritual landscape fits well into a setting of this kind; a flat plain, with standing stones and barrows scattered around. The barrow shown in Illustration 15 though, looks weirdly out of place among the suburban houses. This is the Shrewsbury tumulus and were it not for all the buildings, a clear line of sight would exist from here to the barrow on Plumstead Common. This is the only barrow left of a group which stood in a line along this part of Shooters Hill on the false horizon which would be seen by those on the flat land below. Five of the barrows here were simply razed when the Laing Estate was built here in the 1930s. There was another barrow in a nearby park, but what has become of that, nobody knows. It is, at any rate, no longer visible.

London is, in general, a pretty flat place. There are hills and ridges of high ground, but because there are so many buildings in London, it is often hard to appreciate these parts of the city and fully to realize that before the city was built, such peaks would have been very prominent. Parliament Hill, on Hampstead Heath, is one such high point, from which impressive views may be obtained across the whole of London. In the streets below though, Parliament Hill is hidden from sight. The same applies to Shooters Hill, where Shrewsbury Barrow is situated. It rises to 433ft, which makes it one of the highest points in the Greater London area, and yet it cannot be seen from almost any of the streets in London. Four thousand years ago though, anybody down by the Thames would have been able to glance up and see Shooters Hill and very likely the line of barrows on the side of the hill.

This then is how the communities of that time ensured that prominent or noteworthy people would not be forgotten, that in death, as in life, they would stand out from the crowd. As we have seen, each of these barrows only contained a single burial of either a complete body or the cremated ashes of an individual. It has been suggested that this shift from barrows which contained the remains of a number of people to these single interments tells us something about the changing nature of society at that time, perhaps indicating a less egalitarian approach and one which afforded more significance to leaders. It is unlikely that we shall ever be in a position to prove such a hypothesis.

Continuing along Watling Street towards London, we come to two more sites which tell us about the nature of London during the Bronze Age. The track from Dover led west, until it eventually reached modern-day Greenwich Park. We find here another clue relating to the possible ritual landscape which covered London thousands of years ago.

Greenwich Park is surprisingly wild and hilly for somewhere so close to the centre of London. On a spur of land near a place called One Tree Hill are earthworks which are all that remains of a Romano-Celtic temple which once stood here, beside Watling Street. Watling Street ran just a few yards from this site, which meant that anybody arriving in London from this direction would have been sure to pass the temple. In Roman times, those travelling from Dover to London would have come across this temple before they reached the city itself. In Illustration 16 we see what remains of the site today. This temple is relevant to our exploration, because the Romans did not simply build their temples at random, wherever the mood took them. They rather took over existing places of worship and adapted them for their own purposes. In short, just as the Neolithic folk had continued to venerate sites which were special to the Mesolithic hunters, and the men and women of the Bronze Age took over Neolithic sites and used them, so too did the Romans continue this practice. Indeed, 500 years later, the Saxon invaders did precisely the same thing, as we shall see.

A classic example of this process of continuing veneration of a religious site over the course of thousands of years may be seen in the Essex town of Harlow, which lays a few miles north of London. It was long known that a Roman temple had once stood on the banks of the River Stour, near Harlow, but it was not until a through excavation of the site was carried out that the true nature of the place became apparent. Beneath the Roman temple was found the remains of an early shrine, one dating from the Iron Age and built around 200 or 300 years before the Roman conquest of Britain. This was not surprising, because the concept of continuity of use of such sites is a familiar one. What was a little unexpected though was the discovery of a Bronze Age barrow, which lay beneath the Iron Age shrine and predated it by perhaps a thousand years. Urns containing the ashes of human cremations were found buried within this barrow. Beneath this, an even earlier site was found, associated with the Mesolithic Era, which ended 7,000 years ago. There was one more twist to the story of the Romano-Celtic temple and that was the evidence for the further use of this spot of ground at the end of the fifth century, almost a hundred years after the Romans left. It seemed that Saxon settlers had recognized the importance of this place and built a temple of their own on top of the remains of the Roman temple. In this instance, the continuity of use of a special site lasted for well over 5,000 years. The significance of this will become clear shortly.

The fact that a Romano-Celtic temple stood by Watling Street at this point in Greenwich Park probably means that there was an earlier shrine on the spot and that it was connected in some way with the other parts of the ritual landscape at which we have been looking. This possibly is strengthened by the fact that a short distance away, overlooking Watling Street in fact, is a barrow field, perched on top of a steep hill.

We see in Illustration 11 a bizarre and unfamiliar view of the skyscrapers of Docklands, on the Isle of Dogs. The contrast could hardly be greater. This is a grassy hilltop, covered in ancient burial mounds. The shining towers of 21st-century London provide an incongruous backdrop. There are over thirty barrows on this high ground, most of them little more than slightly raised bumps in the turf. Some have been excavated and the remains found within dated to the time of Saxon London, between 1,000 and 1,500 years ago. However, we know that each new wave of invaders adapted the existing ritual landscape of England for their own purposes, and it is strongly suspected that the Saxons simply appropriated and reused a field of existing Bronze Age barrows for their own burials. This is precisely what was done at the Romano-Celtic temple in Harlow of course. There is excellent reason though, in the case of the Saxons, to suppose that their use of Bronze Age ritual sites was not just the usual case of continuity of use, which we have discussed, but was rather motivated by a deeper affinity with the people who lived in Britain before the Roman invasion. In other words, it may be that the Bronze Age society of Britain had a common belief-system with the Saxons who came here after the Romans left.

In 1922, what is now the east London suburb of Dagenham was a small village in Essex. A huge new housing development was being constructed nearby, on the edge of Goodmayes. This was to become known as the Becontree Estate. It was designed to relieve pressure on the slums of the East End and allow many working-class people to be relocated on the edge of the countryside. Obviously, such a venture would require services such as water, sewage and electricity, and so many deep trenches were being dug in the marshy land near the Thames. In one of these excavations, a curious figure was unearthed.

The Dagenham Idol, as it is now known, may be seen in Illustration 17. It is about 18in high and carved from the wood of a Scots Pine. For many years, it was assumed that this figure probably dated from the Iron Age, a few centuries before the Roman conquest of Britian, but when the carbon dating technique was carried out, a surprise was in store. The Dagenham Idol was actually over 4,000 years old, meaning that it had been made around 2250 BC. It was produced on the very cusp of the beginning of the Bronze Age, making it among the earliest representations of a human figure in Europe.

At first sight, the Dagenham Idol is not an especially inspiring item, its appearance being crude and barely recognizable as a representation of the human form. It looks like something a child might make. Closer study though reveals something very interesting indeed, which allows us perhaps to glean a deeper understanding of a pre-literate society than one would imagine possible. Because although when this wooden figure was made, it would be thousands of years before the art of writing was introduced to this country, we can hazard a guess as to its identity and it is one familiar to us all. So familiar in fact, that one of the days of the week is named after the figure represented by the Dagenham Idol.

There can be no possible doubt that the Dagenham Idol was of great significance, nor that it was deliberately buried as a form of religious ceremony. It was not some grotesquely carved plaything or anything of that sort. We can be confident of this, partly because it was buried so deeply in the ground, in a hole which was 10ft deep and also because of what was buried with it. This was the skeleton of a red deer. Animals with horns and antlers had some special association with the religious practices of the people living in this country during the Bronze Age. That the Dagenham Idol was deposited in a very deep hole, alongside a deer, tells us that this was a sacrificial offering of some kind. Before seeing why we can be so confident about this, a few words may not come amiss about those settlers in Britain who ushered in the Bronze Age.

The descendants of the Yamnaya who settled in Europe, brought with them, in addition to their custom of raising mounds over their dead, a particular set of myths and beliefs in the supernatural, as well as various superstitions. Some of these are so deeply rooted in our lives today, that we never stop to consider where and how such ideas might have arrived in Britain. Take, just for one example, the significance of the number three and also the associations which we have in our minds between left and right.

It was mentioned earlier that in the culture of the Yamnaya people, the number three has seemingly a special significance. Their society was divided into three types; farmers, warriors and priests. This was not the only situation in which the number three cropped up. When we are about to perform some task in unison with others, such as lifting a heavy object, we do not say, 'On the count of four!' or two or five or any other number. It is always three. If we wish to initiate some action, a race for children, for instance, we might typically say, 'One, two, three, go!' Three is so deeply embedded into our consciousness, that we scarcely notice it. In the earliest mythology, we know that there are three fates, three graces and three Norns. The nature of the God, at least according to European theologians, is a trinity. Old fairy stories tell of men being granted three wishes. There is every reason to suppose that this mystical importance of the number three arrived in Europe with the Yamnaya or Indo-Europeans.

Then too, in European culture there has always been a negative association with the left hand and a wholesome and good feeling about the right hand. The word 'sinister', for instance, is derived from the Latin word for the left-hand side. This feeling about the left-hand side being connected with darkness and undesirable things is universal. One plausible explanation is that as the Yamnaya moved into Europe, they oriented themselves not by means of north and south, as we do today, but rather by facing back towards the homeland from which they had emigrated. East was therefore their cardinal direction. Because these people were essentially wanderers and explorers, they were probably aware that the further north one went, the harsher and colder were the conditions, as opposed to the south, which led to balmy and temperate areas. While facing east, this would lead naturally to an association with the right-hand direction being more favourable than that to the left.

Those who crossed the English Channel 4,000 years ago, brought with them all manner of cultural baggage of this kind. The ones who remained in northern Europe and were never part of the Roman Empire continued to adhere to their traditional belief system in its original and unadulterated form, while for those who came under the influence of Rome, the mythology became adapted more to that of Greece. This is because the Romans looked to Greece for their pattern of what represented a cultured and civilized way of life and so used versions of the Greek pantheon as the foundation of their own religion. Those who did not fall under the sway of Rome though, maintained the religious system of the Yamnaya in a more unadulterated form. In exactly the same way, of course, Indo-European language is to this day found in its purest and most unadulterated form in Lithuania, which was historically something of a backwater in Europe.

So, who or what does the Dagenham Idol represent? There are two clues. The first lies in the sexual ambiguity of the figure. Looking at Illustration 17, it will at once be seen that there is a large, round hole between the legs of the figure. This immediately suggests a female, with the hole being a stylised vagina. There is another possibility though, which is that into this hole could be plugged an outsized wooden penis, thus converting the Dagenham Idol into a male. The second clue lies in the crude carving of the face. The right eye is well formed and distinct, but it seems that the left eye was left unfinished and there is a suggestion of deliberate damage being inflicted upon it. This is a curious feature of other, similar figures which have been unearthed in northern Europe, for example the Broddenbjerg Idol from Denmark.

This dates from around 500 BC and its eyes too are fashioned in the same way, that is to say that the right eye is fully formed, but the left is indicated merely by an incised line. Unlike the Dagenham Idol, that from Broddenbjerg has an enormous penis, leaving nobody in any doubt as to its sex.

Putting these clues together gives us a very good idea about the identity of the Dagenham Idol. It is a fair assumption that it represented a deity of some kind, either male or female. Taken in association with other figures, such as that from Broddenbjerg, there is strong suggestion of sexual ambiguity about this character. Adding to this the fact that only one eye seems to be good and intact, indicates that what we are seeing here is the prototype for the Norse god Odin; sometimes also known as Woden. From this latter name is of course derived Wednesday; Woden's day.

Odin, the chief of the gods and goddesses after whom four of our days of the week are named, was known to adopt female form sometimes and even to have sex with men when manifesting in this way. He also practised sorcery, which was thought to be a feminine art and somehow unmanly. Most significantly though, he had only one eye. So determined had Odin been to obtain wisdom that he visited the magic well of Mímisbrunnr and plucked out one of his eyes and cast it into the water as payment for taking a draught from the well. It was thus that Odin became wisest of the gods. Once again, we come across the idea of sacrificing something valuable to us by casting it into a body of water.

Not only was Odin a practitioner of magic, which automatically made his sexuality questionable, he was also a shapeshifter. In some Norse legends, it is said that Odin turned himself into a woman and actually had sex with men, whom he allowed to penetrate him. This would fit in perfectly with the idea of a detachable penis, which the Dagenham Idol evidently featured. It would enable worshippers to venerate the god as either a man or woman, depending upon circumstance.

If, as seems likely, the Dagenham Idol is meant to be an early incarnation of Odin, then it would certainly explain why the Saxons who came to Britain following the end of the Roman occupation, felt some affinity for the temples and tombs which they encountered here. This may perhaps shed light on the Saxon barrow field at which we looked, perched on a hill overlooking the site of that Romano-Celtic temple and also just above Watling Street.

That the Dagenham Idol is so old and was made at the beginning of the Bronze Age, indicates that the people who colonized Britain at that time and replaced the farmers who were already living here, brought with them a particular set of religious beliefs. That one of these related to a hero or god who had lost or sacrificed one of his eyes, seems clear. Since we read stories of a deity who was obviously connected with this image, and since the main flow of cultural ideas from Europe was westwards into Britain, rather than the other way round, it is a fair guess that a one-eyed god was known of in parts of northern Europe 3,000 or 4,000 years ago and that his worship reached the London area via ships which sailed along the Rhine, across the North Sea and then up the Thames.

Thinking now about the burial of things as a way of dedicating them to the gods, which we assume was the case with the Dagenham Idol, leads us back to the subject of votive offerings, which we touched upon earlier. Many weapons, tools, pieces of metal, bits of jewellery and so on have been found in rivers, lakes and bogs, but some such articles have been unearthed after being deliberately buried in the ground. It is generally thought that these too are sacrificial offerings, although an alternative explanation has recently been advanced for what is seen.

Hoards of metalwork have been found all over Britian, dating chiefly from the Bronze Age. Sometimes, the metals involved are silver and gold, and at others, bronze. For instance, gold torcs, a type of elaborate ring to fit around the neck, have been found and also other objects made of gold. These have all, just like the Dagenham Idol, been deliberately buried in holes dug in the ground. There have also been many discoveries of large quantities of bronze objects, similarly concealed in the ground. Some experts believe these hoards to be religious in nature, that is that they have been buried in the same way that some things have supposedly been flung in the water, as a way of giving them to the gods of the underworld.

In 2018, one of the largest hoards of bronze items buried in this way ever found in Britain came to light in the London Borough of Havering. Gravel was being excavated in Rainham, an area next to the Thames and only three miles west of where the Dagenham Idol was found. A total of 453 bronze items were found, including axe heads, swords, spearheads, ingots and various tools. Most had been damaged in some way, either by blunting the edges of the swords or breaking the objects into pieces. It was the third largest hoard of Bronze Age metal of this kind ever found in Britain. The style of the axes and swords dated this discovery to around 800 BC.

Various theories have been devised to account for the Bronze Age hoards and it is entirely possible that there is not one single explanation for the phenomenon and that the reasons for the practice changed and mutated over the centuries. So why might somebody have buried that enormous amount of bronze in east London almost 3,000 years ago?

Apart from the possibility that digging a hole and putting a lot of valuable metal into it might have been done for religious purposes, it is of course quite reasonable to suppose that the owner had simply put it in the ground to keep it safe. In a world without banks, with no locks on doors and without a police force, theft of something worth as much as hundreds of pieces of bronze must have been a very real danger. What better way of keeping your treasure safe than digging a hole in a remote and out of the way location and then just leaving your stash there? Perhaps this was the stock of a trader or smith, who wished to keep his goods securely while he went away for a few days. Maybe he fell victim to an accident and the secret of his hoard died with him. This is probably at least as likely as making an offering to the gods of so much bronze.

Then too, if there was too much bronze circulating in Britain, it might make sense to remove some from the market, creating an artificial shortage and thus driving up the price. Such manipulation of commodity markets is far from unknown in the modern world. A commercial motive for the practice would also account for the way in which the deposition of such hoards of bronze came to an end around 700 BC. It may be true that at times the market in Britain became saturated with bronze, so to speak, thus bringing down the price, but in 800 to 700 BC, new markets emerged in Europe, especially near the Mediterranean. There was now a limitless demand for the copper being produced from the mine at Anglesey. The buyers in Europe preferred to buy the bronze in the form of ingots and so instead of burying old weapons and tools in the ground, they were melted down and shipped overseas. It is likely that that rather than there being a single, overarching explanation for the hoards of metal found, which date from this time, there are probably half a dozen, all of which were motivations for the practice at one time or another.

We have seen that during the Bronze Age, the various earthworks and monuments in London were added to, to the extent that almost all that we can now see of the prehistoric ritual landscape dates from that time, rather than the Neolithic. But apart from religion and funerary monuments, how did the people of London live? What would we have seen if we had visited Bronze Age London?

Of one thing we may be sure, there was no sort of town, or even village, where London stands today. We shall be seeing later one or two places in Greater London which may well have been substantial settlements, where a number of families lived cheek by jowl, but these are all some way from central London. In central London, where the Romans began their city, evidence has only been found of isolated farms and individual huts, rather than any kind of community. In Bermondsey, for example, near London Bridge railway station, an excavation found traces of agricultural activity dating back 3,000 years. There were the marks of an ard, an early type of plough, which had scratched marks in the soil, furrows in which seeds would have been planted.

The landscape of Bermondsey and Southwark was a group of islands, separated by mud flats and streams. Illustration 9 gives some idea of this. There are a few remnants of this lost world to be found, but one needs to hunt for them carefully. Near Guy's Hospital is a road called Great Maze Pond. This is an odd street name, but it was at one time really a pond, where horses and cattle were taken to drink. Running parallel to the approach to Tower Bridge on the south bank of the Thames is Horselydown Lane. Nearby is a very old flight of stairs leading down to the river. These are the Horselydown Old Stairs and the name 'Horselydown' tells us that an area of grazing land was found here, which stretched along nearby Tooley Street, towards what is now London Bridge Station. Horses and cattle were pastured here and they drank from the maze pond. This is an indication of the watery conditions in this part of London, at one time. It was crisscrossed by rivers and streams, with ponds scattered about on the grassy parts.

A fragment of one of the rivers which ran through Bermondsey may still be seen to this day. The name of Bermondsey itself, as was mentioned earlier in this book, is derived from the fact that it was an 'eyot', meaning a small island. Walking east along the bank of the Thames from Horselydown Old Stairs will bring you, after a couple of hundred yards or so, to an inlet of the River Neckinger, which once flowed through Bermondsey and entered the Thames at this point. It has mostly been culverted over and buried beneath the streets, but here you may see one of the many rivers and streams which once divided this part of London into a network of little islands.

Going off at a slight tangent, there is, a little way to the east, another visible part of one of the rivers which once crisscrossed the whole of London, on both sides of the Thames. Just to the west of Greenwich is the River Ravensbourne, a part of which is still open water. It cuts through the chalk plateaus to the north and enters the Thames at Deptford. These two small sections of rivers are all that now remains of the watercourses which were once such a major feature of the topography of this part of Britain.

This part of London was then, right up to a few centuries ago, rich agricultural land. During the Bronze Age, crops were grown here, and livestock pastured. No doubt farmers lived near to the fields they tended, but their homes have vanished without trace. The reason for this is not hard to divine. The roundhouses of that time, and also those of the Iron Age which succeeded that period, were made of untreated wood, straw, earth, clay and dung. In the modern parlance, we would describe such dwellinghouses as being altogether biodegradable. This means that after a certain length of time, they would simply decay and be absorbed into their surroundings, leaving no noticeable remains. Sometimes, there might be a line of detritus to indicate the line of the walls, bits of stone, bones and so on, but of the wood and straw, nothing would be left. The only lasting sign might perhaps be the postholes of the hut, which are sometimes detectable during an archaeological excavation. Of the roundhouse itself though, nothing is to be seen.

The technique used to build a roundhouse is interesting, because it reminds us of something which was remarked upon earlier in this book, which is that the type of buildings which appear in an area reflect the geology there. The roundhouses of Bronze Age and Iron Age London are a perfect illustration of this point.

At Chysauster, in the English county of Cornwall, are the remains of an Iron Age village, which is a couple of thousand years old. It is made up of roundhouses, but because there is so much stone near the surface in that part of Britain, it was this which was used for the walls and paths of the village. Similarly, the Neolithic village of Skara Brae, in the Orkney Islands, is still standing. It too was built of readily available stone. Those living in the Thames Valley were not so fortunately and they had to make do with what building materials were to be found there. For this reason, their own roundhouses were made of limewashed wattle and daub. Although most readers have probably come across these expressions before, they may perhaps not know what precisely is signified by them and so a few words of explanation will probably not come amiss.

The 'wattle' in wattle and daub is simply springy and supple saplings and branches, which are planted in the ground and then woven together to form what will become the outer wall of the hut. There was certainly no shortage of young trees in the London area at the time that roundhouses were the standard type of house. Onto this frame would be daubed mud, clay and even animal dung. This was moistened until it was smooth and more easily worked. This process would be undertaken on both sides of the woven substrate. It is worth mentioning at this point that this is the same raw material is used across large parts of the world, both in the past and also today. In the Americas, the earth is moulded into bricks and known as adobe. Huts in some parts of sub–Saharan Africa are even to this day built in much the same way as Bronze Age, British roundhouses.

Fortunately for the builders, clay is found near to the surface, and earth mixed with clay is an ideal medium for hut building. There is one great disadvantage to the use of mud in this way as a building material, and that is of course that a shower of rain is likely to wash it away. This too is where London's geological makeup comes to the rescue. As we know, not only is there a vast quantity of clay, which would come in handy during the Industrial Revolution for making bricks, but there is also plenty of chalk. As has been previously described, there are still the remains of chalk mines in south London, some of them dating back a very long time. Flints are often found embedded in chalk and that is one reason for digging such mines, but chalk itself is a very useful substance and it was used for building roundhouses.

Chalk is nothing more than an insoluble solid, calcium carbonate. If it is heated though, it turns into calcium oxide. Add water and this becomes calcium hydroxide, more commonly known as slaked lime. From this, one can produce a solution known as limewash. If limewash is painted over plaster or clay, then in time, it will react with rainwater, which is dilute carbonic acid, and the calcium hydroxide will be converted back into calcium carbonate, which is insoluble and will render the 'daub' waterproof.

This excursion into ancient building techniques has been necessary to enable readers to visualize the scene during the Bronze Age and to imagine what they might have come across; had they been walking about at that time near the River Thames.

This was an era where the trend was very much to live in small family groups, rather than villages or towns. There is of course an excellent reason for this. The lifestyle and economy of the time was agrarian. People tended their flocks and grew their crops. Doubtless they traded with each other, but it is unlikely that many people, other than perhaps smiths, made a full-time living out of commerce and trade. A trip around the countryside outside London will, even to this day, show a similar pattern. Fields and woods, with scattered farmhouses here and there. True, there are villages and towns, but these are only possible because they are inhabited by people who do not make their living from farming. They are commuters, who travel to a city or town to work, shopkeepers, garage mechanics, and various other trades. When everybody is farming, then each family needs a good deal of room around their home. It does not make any sense for farmhouses to be crowded together. The only circumstance in which such a thing might occur would be for defence, if there was an external threat. Otherwise, with no shops and few tradespeople, such an arrangement would not be at all convenient.

This then is the reason why no large settlement has been uncovered in London dating from this time. Villages were few and far between, and very small. The plough marks found in Bermondsey, which are from roughly 1000 BC, show that in South London at least, the land was being farmed. Later, two small towns, scarcely larger than modern villages were established in the area now embraced by Greater London, but neither was near central London. Perhaps because it was agricultural land or possibly because of some religious taboo, the district around the ford at Westminster remained clear of human habitation.

The way of life in the Thames Valley changed in various ways as the Bronze Age came to an end, which happened a little over 2,500 years ago. The lifestyle of the whole of Britain gradually changed at this time, but there is good reason to suppose that these changes began in what is now south London. Once again, it was the geology of London which was inextricably bound up with this new way of life and led to the focus of innovation in Britain shifting to the area which would, with the coming of the Romans, become the first real city in Britain.

Chapter 6

A New Kind of Metal

It is traditional and convenient to divide the history of prehistoric Britain neatly into discrete periods. First was the Palaeolithic, then the Mesolithic and Neolithic, followed by the Bronze Age and finally the Iron Age. Of course, history does not really consist at all of such compact and self-contained lengths of time and any individual person living in Britain thousands of years ago would not have seen any but the faintest and subtlest changes in his lifetime. Nevertheless, we can say with assurance that there was a time in London's history when swords, spears and axes were being made of bronze and that at a later date, such weapons and tools were instead forged of iron and steel. There is reason to suppose, backed up by physical evidence, that Britian's Iron Age actually began in London. Before looking at the site which suggests that this may be the case, perhaps we should think a little about why there *was* an Iron Age.

For about 1,500 years, the metal used in this country for everything from swords and axes to hairpins and needles, was bronze. This alloy was hard, enduring and malleable. It could be cast in moulds or hammered into thin sheets, suitable for making helmets and shields. It was pleasant to look at and could be polished until it resembled gold. It is not, at first sight, easy to see why people would abandon the use of this metal for iron. In other words, what advantages, if any, did iron have over bronze?

It is sometimes said that iron is stronger or harder than bronze and that for this reason it was logical for people in prehistoric Britain to switch to using it, but this is not true. A good and well-proportioned alloy of copper and tin is every bit as tough as iron. Not only that, but it has several points to recommend it over iron. For one thing, working at the sort of temperatures which are possible with a basic charcoal furnace, bronze can be heated above its melting point. This means that it is possible to cast anything you wish in bronze, using the *sire perdu*, or lost wax method. This entails making a model of the desired object out of wax and then covering it with soft clay. If this clay is then fired in a kiln, then it will harden and the wax will run out. There is now a hollow mould which can be filled with liquid bronze. This is not possible with iron at the temperatures which were being attained in furnaces in this country before the Roman conquest of Britain. Then too, bronze is far more attractive to look at, with its mellow, golden colour, as opposed to the dull grey of iron. Bronze does not rust or corrode either. At worst, it develops a pale green patina, whereas iron rusts away in damp conditions. Three-thousand-year-old bronze swords have been recovered from British rivers and they look as perfect now as when they were forged. The same cannot be said for iron weapons from prehistoric Britain, which are usually so rusted as to be wholly unrecognizable today. There seems, from these and other considerations, little to recommend iron over bronze. The answer to this conundrum is simple enough and, as we shall see, comes down to a matter of economics.

One of the earliest sites identified in Britain as being definitely associated with the extraction of iron from its ores lies in London. It is possible that the London area was, in a sense, where the Iron Age began in this country. There are several reasons that this might have been so. Before going any further, we need to return to the subject of Chapter 1, which was the geology of London. The replacement of bronze by iron in the lives of prehistoric communities in Britain took place chiefly for one very good reason, which relates to the availability of the raw materials necessary to produce metals in the required quantities. There were other advantages of course to switching from bronze to iron and steel, but this was the main one.

Bronze is an alloy of copper and tin. The ores, that is to say the rocks containing these metals, are not found everywhere. Tin, for example, is very common in Cornwall, but rarer than hen's teeth in some other parts of Britain. Copper too is found in profusion in some parts of North Wales, but not in the Thames Valley. Not only this, but the rocks themselves have to be dug up from the ground, in other words mined. In Cornwall, tin could be found too in streams, in much the way that gold can sometimes be panned for to this day in some parts of the world. In short, getting hold of copper and tin was a time-consuming and difficult enterprise and impossible to undertake other than in certain small geographical areas. A man in the Thames Valley who wanted a quantity of copper or tin would be obliged to obtain the metals from hundreds of miles away.

The difficulty of getting hold of these metals for most people meant that bronze was something of a luxury, even during the Bronze Age itself. This was not at all the case with iron, which from around 700 BC started to become so plentiful that farmers even used it for their agricultural implements. The reason for this is that iron ore is all over the place and it is not necessary to go trekking off to remote parts of the country to find it. Nor is it always found deep underground. In London, iron ore may be found quite literally laying around. Indeed, iron is the most abundant metal in Britain. In other words, it was the ready availability of iron ore which prompted its increasing use in this country from around 700 BC, rather than any inherent superiority of one metal over the other.

In Chapter 5 we looked at a Bronze Age barrow on Shooters Hill in south London. This was one of a group of half a dozen or so, the others have long since disappeared under a housing estate. Near to the Shrewsbury Barrow as it is known, is Eaglesfield Park, where a barrow stood until the 1930s and also where traces of Bronze Age structures have been found. This has led to its being tentatively identified as a ritual site. A recurring theme in this book has been the concept of continuity of use, whereby some location once held a mysterious meaning which lingered on and was handed down through successive generations for centuries and sometimes thousands of years. It is possible that Eaglesfield Park, in the London Borough of Greenwich, is just such a place.

In July 2007, an excavation was undertaken at Eaglesfield Park sponsored by the television programme *Time Team*. During the Second World War, barrage balloons had been tethered here, as part of measures to protect the capital against enemy bombers which were navigating their way along the Thames towards London. It was the site of these balloons which was to be investigated for the television documentary. In the course of the digging though, something a lot more interesting was found on the side of Shooters Hill than some detritus from the Second World War. Buried deep within the ground was found 63kg of iron slag; the discarded products which remain after iron ore has been smelted in a furnace and the metal itself extracted from the rocks.

This part of south London has deposits of a mineral called siderite, which is a carbonate of iron. If these rocks are broken up or crushed and heated to high temperatures by burning charcoal, then it is possible to produce a spongy mass of iron, which must then be hammered to remove impurities. A setup of this kind is known as a bloomery. The heat generated in such primitive furnaces is not sufficient to turn the iron into a liquid, so it is not possible to cast the metal as can be done with copper and bronze. This was a minor consideration though. Having a ready supply of raw materials for the production of iron meant that convenience triumphed over other factors. Although an important consideration, ready availability was not the only reason for switching to iron as the favoured material out of which to fashion things intended for day-to-day use, such as bridle-bits for horses, knives, nails and a host of other things.

It is true that weapons and decorative items produced from bronze could be made very beautiful. It was possibly to polish, engrave fine lines and chase patterns on bronze and also to use inlays of coloured glass, further to enhance the article. Illustration 13 shows a bronze shield, found in the Thames at Battersea, which is an absolute marvel of fine workmanship. It is a pleasing colour, looking like old gold. Swords and daggers produced from bronze are similarly attractive in appearance. This is all well and good for high-value helmets, shields and other war-gear, those made to look good and impress others with their outward appearance, but when it came to practical use, iron and steel were better suited for things like ploughshares, axes and swords. They may have looked rougher, but they possessed the cardinal virtue of being cheaper, as the raw materials needed to produce them lay close at hand. They possessed another quality, which we shall shortly come to. Bronze, though, continued to be used well into the Iron Age for especially important items. The shield in Illustration 13 was made 300 or 400 years after the smelting of iron began in Britain.

The smelting of iron and turning the metal into useful things began in the Middle East and gradually spread west into Europe. By 750 BC the forging of iron was being undertaken by the Celts of central Europe and the idea rapidly crossed the North Sea and became a practice in Britain. It is perhaps no coincidence that it should have been in the Thames Valley that some of the earliest evidence of the smelting or iron has been found. As we know, the River Thames faces the Rhine and this meant that those wishing to carry either goods or ideas from the heart of Europe to Britain, had a ready-made highway. Simply sail along the Rhine from what is now Switzerland or Germany and then carry straight on across the North Sea to the Thames estuary. From there, the tide will give some assistance to your journey, until you reach London. In this way, the concept of smelting iron would be carried in the most natural way, right into the heart of Britain.

Once people living in that part of Britain heard about this new kind of metal-working, it would not perhaps take all that long before they began casting around and wondering if there were any nearby rocks which might yield iron. Lo and behold, on the slopes of Shooters Hill are clays which contain siderites, a perfect source of iron. It would be simply a matter of digging down to expose more of these useful deposits and then setting up a furnace. The word 'furnace' today conjures up images of Bessemer converters and complicated industrial equipment, but in 700 BC nothing of the kind was needed. The 'furnace' was no more than a hole in the ground, piled high with charcoal. All that was required to produce iron and steel was a supply of rocks containing iron compounds, a lot of wood and a good deal of muscle power to work bellows and wield a hammer.

To generate the heat needed to extract metal from ores, a charcoal fire was needed. Roughly 4kg of charcoal are needed for every kilogram of iron which is smelted. Producing charcoal entails converting wood into charcoal by burning it in the absence of oxygen. This will result in the brittle, black substance which we use for sketching. It burns with a much fiercer heat than wood and produces very little smoke as it does so. Building a furnace was not a complicated matter and could be undertaken very easily in the right conditions. On the side of Shooters Hill, there was a plentiful supply of iron ore, and also many trees which could be turned into charcoal. There was also another useful substance, which was just lying a few feet under the topsoil and waiting to be used. This was clay. By great good fortune, the iron ore known as siderite occurs as part of beds of clay. Everything necessary to smelt iron was therefore to be found in the same place. This, incidentally, is why the Weald, the high land to the south of London had such a thriving industry in smelting iron during the medieval period. The geology of Shooters Hill is similar in some ways to that of the Weald, which lies just a few miles south of Greenwich.

To construct a bloomery of the kind found in Eaglesfield Park, one begins by digging a shallow hole with a diameter of a yard or so. Then, blocks of clay are excavated from a trench and, while still wet, built into a cylinder around the hole. This will end up looking like, and functioning as, a chimney. It will be 4 or 5ft high. A hole is left at the base of the chimney. All that is then required is to fill this structure with charcoal, and the iron-bearing stones from which you wish to extract the metal. Then, the charcoal is lit and air from bellows blown through the hole at the base of the furnace to make the flames burn hotter. A furnace of this kind used with copper ore will generate sufficient heat to cause the metal to melt and run out of the rocks in a pure and liquid form. Iron though has a melting point which is some 500 degrees Celsius higher than copper, and what will be produced under these circumstance is an amorphous semi-solid which is known as bloom. This consists of iron, mixed with many impurities, known as slag. This lump must then be hammered flat on an anvil, to beat out all the slag, until only the pure metal remains.

This then, according to the evidence uncovered, was the type of activity undertaken at the site on Shooters Hill. It was not a particularly time-consuming process, building the furnace and firing it could all be undertaken in a single day, as has been demonstrated in modern times by those emulating the extraction of iron from its ores by using only the technology available 2,500 years ago.

We have so far limited our discussion only to comparing the rival merits of bronze and iron as regards appearance and strength, which shows that the two metals are pretty evenly matched as far as utility is concerned and that indeed, bronze is superior when it comes to durability and external appearance. It has two disadvantages though, both minor in themselves but which are significant when considering weapons like swords and tools such as ploughshares. One of these is that a given volume of bronze is heavier than its equivalent in iron. A cubic foot of bronze weighs 541lb, compared with 480lb for wrought iron. This may not seem significant, but when one is wielding a long sword, lightness, sharpness and strength are crucial. Bronze suffers from another fault, which is that when given a sharp enough blow, it is apt to fracture, which is something which will never happen with an implement made of wrought iron. A broken sword during a battle can be a disaster for a warrior, which is one reason why swords were increasingly made of iron and steel.

Iron was better suited for very rough purposes when it came to agriculture, as well as warfare. The soil in and around London, especially north of the Thames, is heavy and full of clay. With iron ploughshares, it proved possible in the late Iron Age to start tilling the earth more effectively, which perhaps made the land more productive and supported a greater population. The plough marks found in Bermondsey were made by an ard, which is a primitive kind of plough which really just scratches a deep line in the soil. With an iron ploughshare, it was possible to turn over furrows as we do today, which makes agricultural land a good deal more productive.

The Iron Age is, in a sense, inaptly named, because it was not iron itself which revolutionized the way of life in Europe, but rather the discovery and exploitation of an alloy of iron, one which is incomparably stronger and harder than either iron or bronze. This is steel. There might not be much to choose in sharpness or strength between an iron sword and a bronze one, but both are puny things when compared with a sword which has a tempered steel edge. The Iron Age in Britain was a time of warfare and strife and it can hardly be coincidental that this state of affairs arose at the same time that steel swords were becoming common. New and more effective weapons, whether they are steel swords, cannons or nuclear bombs, have always had the effect of changing the world.

Steel is an alloy of iron and carbon and although somewhat more brittle than iron, is far harder. Only a tiny amount of carbon needs to be added to iron to produce steel, just 1 or 2 per cent, but the effect of that addition is dramatic. Because it proved impossible in prehistoric Britain to raise the temperature of a furnace to such a level as to melt iron, another way had to be found of alloying it with another element. Producing bronze, which is also of course an alloy, presented no problem in this respect, because both copper and tin have low enough melting-points to be turned into liquids in a charcoal furnace. It was simply a matter of adding a certain amount of liquid tin to a crucible of melted copper and ensuring that the mixture was stirred well. Melting pure iron and adding a precisely calculated amount of carbon is of course the ideal method also of producing steel. Because the furnaces lacked sufficient heat for this method to be used, an alternative technique was accordingly devised.

Charcoal is no more than carbon. If an iron sword was heated to red heat and laid for some hours on a bed of glowing charcoal, then some of the carbon would diffuse into the iron, forming a coating of steel. The red-hot sword would then be plunged into cold water, a process known as quenching. This results in a much harder metal. It would have a tempered steel outer layer, with a more flexible iron core.

How did the introduction of iron and steel affect life in the area which we now know as Greater London? It is sometimes difficult to untangle what was caused by something and what might simply have happened shortly after some other development. We must, in other words, be careful not to fall into the logical error of *post hoc, ergo propter hoc*; this happened before this thing, therefore this was the cause of that other thing. This means that we must be cautious about constructing a narrative which may turn out to be an imaginative piece of myth-making, in which steel swords are linked to the rise in a warrior cast and the establishment of hill forts. Such a story may well be pleasing, but it is not necessarily true. So it is that the Iron Age saw both the smelting of iron in the London area and also the growth of larger communities and the building of hill forts. The connection between these two things may not be a direct one.

During the Neolithic and Bronze Age, little evidence has been found in and around London for villages or towns. The pattern of occupation seems to be scattered farms and, at most, the occasional hamlet. Then, about a century after the smelting of iron was being carried out at Shooters Hill, hill forts were being built in south London, the remains of which can still be seen. Readers may be taken aback to discover that there is a hill fort just five and a half miles from the Tower of London, although hardly anybody knows of its existence. Before we look at this site, it might be a good idea to think a little about the nature of hill forts, to see what they were and why they were built.

Shaping the landscape was something undertaken during the Neolithic and Bronze Ages by building countless burial mounds, erecting standing stones, digging cursuses, henges and causewayed enclosures, to say nothing of the piling-up of chalk to create a huge artificial hill, as was done at Silbury on Salisbury Plain. All these efforts led to the construction of ritual landscapes, which were visually striking. In the Iron Age, the chief means of remodelling the land was by means of ditches and banks which were used to surround hilltops and parts of plateaux. This was the age of first the hill fort, and later the oppidum.

Because London is not a notably hilly place, the hill forts to be found there, including the one on Wimbledon Common, might perhaps be more properly described as plateau forts, as they are to be found on flat ground which is only a little higher than the surrounding area, rather than on the crest of a hill, as is often the case elsewhere in Britain. It is the same with the two hill forts in Epping Forest, to the north of London. We shall be looking at these in detail shortly, because they provide an excellent illustration of a puzzle which surrounds such places, which is what they were actually *used* for. Some hill forts obviously contained villages, groups of huts which were permanently occupied. Others though give the impression of only having been used as a place of refuge in times of trouble; somewhere that people went for shelter during an emergency. Archaeological excavations of some such sites reveal no trace of any buildings, just a few groups of four post-holes. It is thought by some that these hill forts might have been used only as stockades for herds of cattle and flocks of sheep, perhaps when they were being rounded up and counted.

The very term hill fort has a martial air to it and puts us in mind of battles and sieges. The defensive earthworks which surround hill forts indicates that they were built to withstand attack, but there are other possible explanations. The keep of the Tower of London is a massively strong structure which would have been very difficult for an enemy to take, but that was not the primary purpose behind its construction. It was designed to look impressive, to be seen from miles around and show anybody passing by that those who were behind this tall, strong tower were people to be feared and respected. It was a symbol of domination and power. This could well have been one of the motives for the hill forts which sprung up during the Iron Age. Those arranging for the excavation of deep ditches, the piling up of banks of earth and the building of wooden walls and palisades, might have been sending a signal to both neighbouring tribes and any casual foreign invaders that here was a stronghold that it would be wise to leave alone.

Another idea which has been floated is that at least some hill forts were really marketplaces, and somewhere that craftsmen worked to produce and sell their wares. There are traces of blacksmiths' forges and loom weights which show that ironwork and weaving were carried on and perhaps the resulting goods sold or bartered in some, but not all, hill forts. The most likely explanation is perhaps that all these possibilities are true in different places and that there was not one single purpose behind the construction of hill forts. The rise of the hill fort, which coincided with the forging of iron swords, not only in London, but also in much of southern Britain at that time, has helped create a fantasy image of warriors and mighty kings.

The fact that two hill forts are to be found only a few miles from the centre of London and that this is not widely known may perhaps be accounted for by the historic snobbishness which many Londoners north of the Thames feel about south London. All the famous landmarks, buildings, institutions and districts are to be found in the City of London and Westminster. To give one example, there can be very few Londoners who have not heard of St Paul's Cathedral. Ask those familiar with Wren's masterpiece about the Cathedral of St Saviour and St Mary Overie, though, or St George's Cathedral, and they will look at you blankly. Where on earth can these cathedrals be found? The answer is that both are in London, but south of the Thames. Little wonder then that few have heard of them!

In Chapter 5 we visited Plumstead Common and Shooters Hill and examined some Bronze Age barrows, which formed part of a ritual landscape. The nearest railway station to those barrows also happens to be the closest to the most impressive hill fort in London. This is a site known as Charlton Camp and it was excavated in 1915.

The area of the south bank of the Thames which lies near the Thames Barrier is not an inspiring place. Put bluntly, it is a patchwork of sites associated with the former industry and maritime trade of London. Many of these so-called 'brownfield' sites are being developed and high-rise blocks of flats built on them. Tucked away in the middle of this district, Charlton, is Maryon Park. Maryon Park was established over a century ago on what used to be a quarry, where sand was extracted for building purposes and glassmaking. Part of the area is still fenced off, because the end-result of the quarrying was a series of steep cliffs, some of them treacherous to walk near, being composed in the main of no more than sand and earth.

The whole of Maryon Park has been carved out of what was once a hill, because the land in this part of London is quite hilly, as we may see when looking at one of the highest points in London, which is nearby Shooters Hill. It was therefore quite logical for those living hereabouts during the Iron Age to choose one of these hills, along the riverside, to turn into a fortified enclosure. The remains of this hill fort are to be seen on Cox's Mount, which is the northernmost part of Maryon Park. Illustration 18 shows the beginning of the flight of steps which leads up the steep slope, to a smooth, grassy plateau.

Although it only rises 70 or 80ft above the level of the nearby Thames, the view from Cox's Mount is impressive, due to the overall flatness of most of this part of the Thames Valley. A semaphore station run by the Admiralty once stood here and signalled to a nearby station on Shooters Hill. This was a part of a chain of such stations which ran from London to Deal, an optical telegraph line which enabled messages to pass from the Admiralty in Whitehall to the harbour in Deal in a matter of seconds. The mount was also a landmark for ships sailing along the Thames; when passing it, those on board knew that Cox's Mount was directly due south.

The summit of Cox's Mount today is a grassy glade, perhaps a little over an acre in area, and surrounded by trees. It was at one time much greater, but the sides have been eroded by the quarrying of sand. This would, before the trees of the park were planted and grew to obscure the view, have been a spectacular viewpoint. There could hardly be a more perfect location for a hill fort. Even today, with all the building work going on in the distance, there is a remote and otherworldly quality about the summit of Cox's Mount. It is true that hardly any trace remains of the fortifications such as the banks and ditches which once ringed the top of the hill, but even so, it is possible to appreciate the strategic importance of this location. This is the closest hill fort to central London and almost completely forgotten today.

The other hill fort which is only a few miles from the centre of London, and may be freely visited, is called Caesar's Camp and it is also in south London, on Wimbledon Common. Until the spring of 1875, Wimbledon Common and the adjacent Putney Heath were part of a ritual landscape dating back to the Bronze Age. More than thirty barrows were dotted about the common and they were overlooked by a marvellously preserved Iron Age hill fort. This was known as Caesar's Camp, although there is no reason at all to associate the place with Julius Caesar. There are other prehistoric sites in Greater London bearing this name. The hill fort at Wimbledon had ramparts which were six yards high, together with a deep ditch which ran around the whole, circular structure. There were views across Epsom Downs from the ramparts. The land was owned by a Member of Parliament called John Samuel Sawbridge-Erle-Drax. He owned a good deal of land in and around Wimbledon. He leased some of it to a builder called Dixon, who began building houses, first having levelled all the barrows. In April 1875, the builder arranged for the hill fort to be levelled and more bricks and mortar were delivered to the site. Eventually, a legal order was obtained to prevent the building of more houses on what was really common land, but it was too late to save Ceasar's Camp. Most of it lies today beneath a golf course and the fragment which remains is barely recognizable, merely an irregularity in the terrain.

This site we know today as Caesar's Camp was occupied for 200 years or so. That it was built near to an extensive field of barrows indicates that this may be yet another instance of continuity of use, a concept which we have examined earlier. In other words, there was something about this patch of high ground which meant something to those who lived here thousands of years ago. It may be significant that the common is almost next to Richmond Park, where both a Neolithic and Bronze Age barrow are still to be found. It may be that this entire region was part of a larger ritual landscape, something akin to Salisbury Plain, although on a smaller scale.

What is noticeable is that none of the hill forts are to be found close to the Thames in north London. There are certainly hills at Hampstead and near Regent's Park, but nobody, it seems, was minded to start any kind of settlement that close to the Thames. South of the river, Cox's Mount and Caesar's Camp are as close as anything of the sort is found. In north London, one needs to go out as far as Epping Forest if you wish to see a hill fort. There are two good examples to be found, hidden away in the forest. The first is called Loughton Camp and lies just a mile from the town of Loughton, which can be reached on the London Underground.

Today, Loughton Camp is hidden away in the depths of dense woodland, but when it was created, in perhaps 500 BC, the land here had been cleared of trees. The fort is on a spur of high ground, the highest for miles around, and would at one time have commanded a view across the whole of the Thames Valley and as far south as Shooters Hill and even the hills of

Surrey behind it. We know this, because on a nearby vantage point, York Hill in Loughton, one can indeed see this far and on a clear day, the whole of London is spread out before one. Illustration 19 shows the view from this high country when it is not obscured by trees. Interestingly enough, Shooter's Hill may be seen from this vantage point, although it lies 15 miles away, on the other side of the Thames.

Loughton Camp consists of a ditch and earth rampart enclosing 12 acres. It is one of two hill forts in Epping Forest, and it has been hypothesised that these belonged to different tribes and might have served as symbolic frontier posts; delineating territory. According to this theory, Loughton Camp would have belonged to the Trinovantes, a powerful group at that time. Given its position, it is possible too that it served as a lookout, enabling a watch to be kept on any approaching threat from the south. It has also been suggested that this imposing fort was really no more than a corral for cattle. The remains today are far from imposing.

Nobody can say how long ago Loughton Camp was built, nor for what purpose. Considering the amount of organization which would have been needed for such an enterprise, this was an important operation. A spring rises in Loughton Camp, making the nearby ground boggy and this would mean of course that once inside the walls, people could have withstood a siege and been self-sufficient in water at least. On the other hand, it might have been just as handy to have a supply of fresh water if the intention was to round up cattle roaming in the area and to confine them here for a while, for some purpose. There is no evidence at all to indicate which theory about the place is the correct one.

One curious point, and this brings us back once more to the concept of continuity of use, is that this part of Epping Forest is far richer in traces of Mesolithic occupation than in evidence of activity during the Iron Age. In other words, the hill fort seems to have been built on a site which was had been important to the hunter-gatherers who lived in the Thames Valley thousands of years before anybody had the idea of finding a good spot for a fortified position. Whether this was because this particular location had some spiritual significance or just because it was the highest bit of ground for miles around, it is impossible to say, but men and women in the Mesolithic era certainly found this a good base. They made flint tools here and this was without doubt somewhere that was returned to time and again.

Although the banks and ditches surrounding Loughton Camp are now smooth and require no great effort to clamber over, it is something of a miracle that they survive at all after 2,500 years. They were, after all, composed originally on nothing more than earth and mud. Few people visit the area, as it is a little way from any main pathway through the forest. So dense are the trees now, that it is difficult to imagine that this would once have been a fantastic viewpoint, allowing people to see right across to the Surrey Hills.

A couple of miles to the north-east is another hill fort of similar construction. This is Amesbury Banks and according to local legend, it is where Queen Boudicca made her last stand. There is, however, absolutely no evidence for this idea. The position of Amesbury Banks is unlikely to have been chosen at random. It is on flat ground, not perched on a high spur, as Loughton Camp is, and at first glance, there is nothing in particular to distinguish this patch of flat ground from any other for a few miles in any direction. We now know though, that this was a strategic point, at least 1,000 years before work began on digging the ditches and banks which go to make up the fortification. This at least seems likely, because a good deal of work went into building what was, in effect, a dam. The work on this dam, which was constructed in order to provide a dry path through a marsh, was carried out 2,000 years before Amesbury Banks was built.

A few hundred yards to the west of Amesbury Banks is a narrow bridle path, which was until 10 years ago, a minor road leading up to a ruined mansion called Copt Hall. This is Lodge Road, so called because it led to the lodge which stood at the gates of Copt Hall. It was closed to traffic some years ago and now forms a pleasant, tarmacked footpath through the forest; a route for pedestrians, cyclists and those on horseback. An interesting feature of the walk along this former road is that on one side is a bog, formed when a couple of streams were dammed by the construction of the road, an event carbon-dated to 2340 BC. Obviously this part of the forest was important enough to warrant the building of a trackway at that time, which means that it is possible that the siting of Amesbury Banks here had some significance behind it of which we are ignorant.

The culmination of the Iron Age in Britain came with what many people think of as the Celtic culture; the people who ruled the country at the time of the Roman conquest. There are many misconceptions about the Celts and since it was their tribal groupings which very likely helped to maintain the Thames as a border and discourage the building of any large settlement upon its banks, the next chapter will be devoted to the Celts, their language, history and culture.

Chapter 7

Celtic London

The last century or two before historical records exist about the part of the Thames Valley at which we have been looking, saw great changes in Britain. When the Romans invaded the country in 43 AD, it was a Celtic nation that they subdued, whatever we understand this to mean. Julius Caesar is explicit about this point when he recorded the two expeditions which he led to Britain in 55 BC and the following year. He claimed that the people with whom he came into contact had only lately arrived in Britain and that they were Celts who had crossed the Channel and established themselves in the south-east of the country. Writing in the *Gallic Wars*, he says,

> The inland portions of Britain are inhabited by those who themselves say that according to tradition they are natives of the soil; the coast regions are peopled by those who crossed from Belgium for the purpose of making war. Almost all of these are called by the names of those states from which they are descended and from which they came hither. After they had waged war they remained there and began to cultivate the soil.

Until relatively recently, this outline of early British history was accepted as fact, and it was thought that a large number of

'Celts' crossed the English Channel during the Iron Age and established chiefdoms or kingdoms in what is now East Anglia, Kent and other parts of South East Britain.

There is no doubt that the culture of South East Britain changed over the course of a few centuries, in the period which immediately preceded the Roman conquest of the country. New customs emerged, including the first towns. Habits such as the drinking of wine became more common and instead of scattered families and clans, confederations of tribes appeared, which meant that a single ruler would hold sway over an area as large as a modern-day county. Then too, these people spoke the same language as those living in parts of mainland Europe such as Gaul. One can readily appreciate why Caesar jumped to the conclusion that all this could best be explained by the invasion of Britain by fierce settlers from Gaul, who had imposed a new lifestyle, language and culture upon the indigenous inhabitants. In other words, the 'Celts' were believed to be a distinct, ethnic group, with a particular language, culture and origin, who somehow expanded from central Europe to occupy a large part of what is now France, Belgium and Britain.

A moment's thought though will soon show the flaws in this line of reasoning. After all, curry is very popular in twenty-first century Britain. This is not evidence of an Indian invasion, but a purely cultural effect. The more international trade and contact a country has, the more chance is there of people acquiring a taste for some food or drink from elsewhere in the world. As we have seen, there was no shortage of trade between Britain and the Continent at this time.

What about the fact that people in Britain that Caesar encountered seemed to speak the same language and have a similar set of customs and traditions to those he had encountered in Gaul? Again, it is hardly necessary to posit an invasion to account for such a state of affairs. Greek was the *lingua franca* of the Mediterranean 2,000 years ago. The Gospels were written in Greek and it was a language spoken by educated people in Rome. This did not mean that Rome had been invaded and occupied by the Greeks, it was a cultural matter.

The people living in Britain were, like those on mainland Europe, the descendants of the Yamnaya who had ushered in the Bronze Age. Obviously, they were likely to speak a similar Indo-European language as the rest of those in Europe, including the culture whom we now know as the Celts. Although an island, Britain was not isolated or cut off from Europe and there was a lot of coming and going across the English Channel. It would have been surprising really if those living in that part of Britain which is now London did *not* speak much the same language as the people in Gaul.

There is no genetic evidence to indicate that large numbers of people migrated to Britain during the Iron Age, but there is, on the other hand, abundant evidence that that part of the country closest to the English Channel and North Sea adopted a very similar lifestyle to that of people in Gaul, but with some distinctive differences. The adoption in Britain of such things as styles of decoration, religious practices and personal names can all be explained by the flow of ideas, rather than the transference of populations from one part of Europe to another.

The latter part of the Iron Age in Britain saw the abandonment of some hill forts and the creation of a new kind of settlement, the oppidum. Once again, we have Julius Caesar to thank for both the word and the information about the lifestyle of some people living in Britain when he visited the country during two military expeditions. Every schoolchild used to know that Caesar invaded Britain in 55 BC, but this was a very short visit, and the Roman forces did not advance inland. They were content to set up camp on the shore and simply remain there, repulsing attacks from angry Britons who mustered an army and tried to drive the invaders back into the sea. The landing took place at the end of August, and it was obvious to Julius Caesar that if he was to have any chance of moving further into the interior, then he would need to return with more men and horses, which he duly did the following year. It is thanks to this later expedition that we know something about the way of life of the British at that time or at least those who lived in the south and east of the country.

After securing his beachhead during the second expedition in 54 BC, Caesar knew that if he wanted to represent his venture as a conquest of some kind, then he would need to strike into the interior of the country and make his presence known, if necessary, by subduing the inhabitants by military force. For this reason, he brought with him on this second visit no fewer than 27,000 infantry and 2,000 cavalry. This time, Caesar was ready for anything.

It is in Caesar's account of this second incursion into Britain that we might perhaps say that the history of London, that is to say a written record of the area, first emerges. The chief power in the land, a king whose influence stretched across a large swathe of south-east Britain north of the Thames, was a man called Cassivellaunus. His tribe, the Catuvellauni, had been pursuing an expansionist policy and overthrowing the rulers of neighbouring confederations such as the Trinovantes. It seemed to Julius Caesar that if he could humble this leader, then he would have stamped his authority upon Britain. To reach the stronghold of the Catuvellauni though, it would first be necessary to cross the Thames. With this in mind, the Roman army marched north, heading for a ford of which they had been told, across the Thames.

The location of the ford by which Caesar and his army crossed the Thames has been much debated. Many people assert that it was at Westminster, since this was the first point on the river which could be forded, if you were heading west from the estuary. It has also been claimed that the ford was at either Brentford, near Kew Gardens, or perhaps at Walton-on-Thames. Wherever the ford was, Caesar and his army fought their way across the Thames and headed north into the heart of the Catuvellauni territory, where there was what Caesar describes in his account of the campaign as an oppidum. Hill forts had by this time fallen from favour and the new centres of population were more likely to be found on level ground, often by a river. Such places were, in effect, the first towns.

The oppidum which was the focus of Caesar's campaign in 54 BC need not concern us overmuch, for it was outside Greater London. It was most likely in Hertfordshire. A more interesting point is why was there no oppidum in the area which the Romans chose as the site of the new city of Londinium a century later? There was a ford, major tracks converged there and iron was being smelted and forged nearby. More than that, the remains have been found of ancient wooden structures, both of which are within a short distance of Westminster and yet there is no sign of anything resembling a town in what is now central London.

Two oppida have been found in Greater London, but neither one of them is near the centre of the city. One lies on the banks of the River Roding in the suburb of Ilford and the other is in Woolwich, a stone's throw from the south terminal of the Woolwich Ferry. There are several possible explanations as to why nobody thought it worth building a large settlement near the ford at Westminster, where Watling Street crossed the Thames. One is that the Thames effectively marked the border between the territory of the powerful Catuvellauni and the tribes who lived south of the river. The area south of the ford and also for some distance to the north, might have been regarded as a demilitarized zone, where, by common consent, nobody would establish any permanent armed camp. Another possibility is that this section of the river was seen as being in some way sacred and that everybody from any tribe would feel safe coming here to make sacrifices into the water of weaponry and so on. We know, both from the early wooden structures which have been found and also because of the astonishing number of valuable artifacts recovered from the water, that the practice of casting things into the Thames here was still going strong, right up to the Roman conquest.

Of the oppidum which was built on the bank of the Thames, far from the ford in central London, we can say little. Traces of it were uncovered during excavations for building work between Beresford Street and the river, in an area which once formed part of the Royal Arsenal at Woolwich. Ditches and banks were found and dated to between the third and first centuries BC. A track once led from here, up to Watling Street, which passed south along Shooters Hill. Nothing more is known about this oppidum, although it has been suggested that it was a port of some kind. Less than two miles to the west lies the remains of an Iron Age hill fort in Maryon Park and we can perhaps hazard an educated guess that the oppidum at Woolwich was constructed at about the time that the hill fort was abandoned; perhaps even as part of a planned replacement. We know that there was a shift from hill forts to oppida at this time and it seems a little too much of a coincidence to find a hill fort and oppidum separated by so small a distance.

A great deal more is known of the other oppidum in the London area, which lay on the banks of the Roding, between the modern districts of Ilford and Barking. This was a most impressive place, covering an area of almost 50 acres. It was, by way of comparison, almost as large as the well-known hill fort of Maiden Castle in Dorset. That such an enormous settlement should lie in a quiet London suburb with hardly anybody having heard of it is little short of incredible.

The reason that so few people, even those living within a few yards of it, are aware of Uphall Camp is that it was for almost the whole of the twentieth century buried beneath streets of Victorian houses on one side and an industrial site on the other. No sooner had the Howards chemical works been demolished, and archaeologists given an opportunity to examine the site, than that part of the oppidum was covered once more in concrete and turned into a new housing estate. All that remains today are some dips in nearby roads which show the line of the ditch and bank which delineated the camp.

Although it was suggested by some antiquaries in the nineteenth century, before building began along the banks of this part of the River Roding, that the earthworks known as Uphall Camp was all that remained of a Celtic fort, little evidence came to light. Once the houses and factory were built, the matter became little more than a piece of local folklore. It was not until the chemical works were first extended and then finally demolished, that it was possible to make any real investigation of what lay there.

The oppidum which we know today as Uphall Camp was built on a gravel island, of the kind which were known on the Thames as eyots. On the west, it was bounded by the Roding and on the south by a small waterway called Loxford Stream. It is not possible even to guess how many people once lived here, in the centuries leading up to the Roman conquest in 43 AD. Nor can we even be sure to what tribe they belonged. Coins have been found here which were minted by the Canti, a tribe south of the Thames which gave their name to the county of Kent and city of Canterbury. From these, and other indications, we can be sure that this settlement was active a century or two before Britain was occupied by the Romans and perhaps for some years after that time. We know too that smelting was undertaken here, because slag has been found. There were traces as well of granaries and huts.

Both Uphall and the oppidum found at Woolwich have a feature which indicates that those who built these proto-towns were not from the Continent but were rather the native inhabitants of Britain. They share this particular way of construction with what is sometimes cited as the oldest town in Britain, which is Colchester.

When the Romans invaded the country in 43 AD, probably the largest settlement was the oppidum called Camulodunon, a name attested from coins dating around 20 BC. The name was later Romanised to Camulodunum. The town's defences were similar to those at Uphall and Woolwich, in that they consisted of low banks, interspersed with ditches. At first sight, this seems a curiously ineffective way of protecting a settlement from a determined assault by enemy forces. So low were the banks and so shallow the ditches, that any agile warrior would have been able simply to scramble over them if he was intent on reaching the homes which these earthworks were supposedly defending. It is a puzzle, until one understands the way that warfare was conducted in Celtic Britain. This in turn sheds light upon the idea mentioned at the beginning of this chapter, which is that the people living in south-east Britain at this time might really have come to the country from Gaul and be in fact recent settlers.

Almost 100 years before Claudius invaded and occupied Britain, Julius Caesar was taken by surprise during his own campaigning in the country, by the fact that the chief tactic relied upon by the Britons was the extensive use of chariots. Writing in the *Gallic Wars*, Ceasar said that;

This is their manner of fighting from chariots. At first the charioteers ride in all directions, usually throwing the ranks into confusion by the very terror caused by the horses, as well as the noise of the wheels; then as soon as they have come between the squads of horsemen, they leap from the chariots and fight on foot. The drivers of the chariots then withdraw a little from the battle and place the chariots together, so that if the warriors are hard pressed by the number of the enemy, they have a safe retreat to their own. Their horsemen possess such activity and their foot soldiers such steadfastness in battle and they accomplish so much by daily training that on steep and even precipitous ground they are accustomed to check their excited horses, to control and turn them about quickly, to run out on the pole, to stand on the yoke, and then swiftly to return to the chariot.

The reason that he described the method of fighting at such length is because he had not before encountered it. The use of chariots on the battlefield was all but unknown in Gaul; this was a peculiarly British mode of warfare. This suggests that far from having emigrated to Britain from Gaul, the people living there had devised their own special ways of fighting and an original tradition had arisen in the country of the chariot as being the main weapon of war.

All of which brings us back to the banks and ditches surrounding the British oppida. The low banks were what are known today as 'berms'. Although the word itself might be unfamiliar to readers, they have almost certainly seen berms. Sometimes farmers wish to prevent travellers from entering a field and setting up their caravans there. The same fear is from time to time felt by local authorities regarding some flat piece of grassland which might be targeted for a temporary encampment. Getting such travellers removed legally can be a long and arduous process and so it has been found that an ounce of prevention is worth a pound of cure. In this case, the prevention consists of digging a shallow ditch and piling the earth up in a bank, which might be no more than a foot or 18in in height. This makes it impossible for a wheeled vehicle to cross. It is precisely the same principle as the berms which surrounded the Celtic oppida in Britain; the aim in their case being to ensure that chariots were unable to come to close to their homes in an attack.

Returning now to the oppidum in Ilford, the fact that Uphall Camp was situated by the side of a river makes it likely that the people who lived here were trading goods to other parts of the Thames Valley. The River Roding flows down to the Thames and would have made it easy to make contact with those in Kent, which accounts perhaps for the discovery of coins from that part of the country. There is reason to suppose that there were strong connections between the people living in this part of London and those across the water in Kent. Discoveries made in the neighbouring district of Dagenham in the 1990s may shed light on this and also give us a new perspective on life in the Thames Valley at that time.

Although we now know that wooden trackways were laid over marshy land in Britain from the Neolithic onwards, most people assume that proper roads did not make their appearance until the Romans arrived. In the last 30 or 40 years though, this has been found to be quite untrue. In 1994 Frank Meddens, an archaeologist with the Passmore Edwards Museum in the London Borough of Newham, gave a newspaper interview, in the course of which he spoke of the earliest properly constructed road in the whole of northern Europe, which had been discovered in Dagenham.

The road unearthed in Dagenham was no mere track or path. It was rather a highway which rivalled that of the Romans in construction. It ran for at least a mile, to the Thames, and was four yards wide. The surface of the road was made of gravel, and it was speculated that cattle might have been driven along it. It would also have been suitable for riders. Why such a road was needed to run to the bank of the Thames in that way is not known. One idea put forth was that it might have led to a ferry which operated between Dagenham and that part of the south bank of the river, which lies between Dartford and Woolwich. Such a connection with what was then the territory of the Canti might possibly account for coins struck there having turned up at Uphall Camp.

We have seen that the land around London was, in the centuries leading up to the Roman conquest, gradually witnessing the emergence of urban settlements. It would perhaps be an exaggeration to call the oppida towns, let alone cities, but that was the direction in which society was moving. In addition to the two oppida at Woolwich and Ilford, smaller villages have been found, including one at Heathrow.

We have already seen that a few Iron Age temples have been found in the Greater London area, but evidence of London as important in a religious sense to the Celts is often indirect, but none the less compelling for that. We start by asking ourselves how much we can actually know about the religion practiced at this time, in this part of Britian, in the years leading up to the Roman conquest in 43 AD. The answer is, quite a lot.

The religion followed by the Romans was largely based upon that of the Greeks. These beliefs, together with those of the Celts, had of course a common source in the culture of the Yamnaya, who triggered the Bronze Age in Europe when they swept in from the plains of what are now Russia and Ukraine. For this reason, we need not be surprised to find similarities between the mythology of the various peoples descended from those invaders, any more than we should be taken aback to find that their languages are related to each other. So it was that when the Romans settled in Britain, they recognized some of the deities venerated by the Celts and saw in them versions of their own gods. It was of course partly for this reason that we see the emergence of Romano-Celtic temples and sacred sites in this country, as stout Roman temples were erected where there were already wattle-and-daub structures built by the local inhabitants. So it is that when they colonized the area of modern-day Bath, in the west of England, the Romans found there hot springs, dedicated to a goddess called Sulis, who was thought to be associated with healing and health. The warm water was presumably thought to be therapeutic, rather like the similar spas which even today are patronised by those in poor health. The Romans saw in Sulis their own goddess of Minerva and so it was that they established a temple and sanctuary to Sulis-Minerva. Something of the kind happened in central London and helps shed light on the status of the area before the Roman city was founded.

Some way south of London Bridge, in that part of south London known as Southwark, some extensive building work was being undertaken in the early part of the present century. It was known that this spot, near Borough Tube station, was where the Roman road of Stane Street ran, as it approached the Thames. The archaeological remains which were found here indicated that this was the site of a large temple complex, consisting of two temples and plinths for a number of statues. There may also have been a guesthouse of some kind. These buildings would have stood by the side of the road, so anybody heading north to London would be obliged to pass them on their way to the city.

We have looked at the concept of continuity of use, that is to say Mesolithic holy places which were also revered by Neolithic farmers and later by the immigrants who ushered in the Bronze Age to Britain. The Romans carried on this practice, of course, and so it is worth asking ourselves if this large complex was established here because there was already a Celtic place of worship nearby. The answer is, almost certainly that was the case.

As well as the remains of the temples themselves, a few fragments were found which shed light upon the origin of these places of worship. The first was a bronze foot, in the form of a cloven hoof. This can only have come from a statue of the woodland god Pan, who is depicted as half human and half goat, with horns on his head. Then too, a marble plaque was unearthed, bearing in Latin an inscription, the translation of which read, 'To the Divinities of the Emperors and to the god Mars Camulus, Tiberius Celaranius, a citizen of the Bellovaci, morotix, of Londoners'. Just as in the case of Sulis–Minerva, we see here a Celtic deity linked with the Roman equivalent from their own pantheon of gods and goddesses. Obviously, a shrine to Camulus stood here and was replaced by a Roman temple to what they assumed was another incarnation of the Celtic god, in this case their own Mars, the god of war.

Camulus was a very popular god in both Britain and across the Channel in Gaul. He is always shown with horns, rather like Pan. It will be recalled that the original name of Colchester was Camulodunon, which means the stronghold of Camulus. The Iron Age Britons, especially in London, seemed to have had an affection for gods and goddesses connected with hunting. We have already seen that a few hundred yards to the north of the Southwark temples, the statue of a god was found in a well. This bears no resemblance to any figure from Roman mythology and is assumed to be a British creation, showing one of their own gods. The huntsman, for this is what he appears to be, is flanked by a stag and a dog, putting some people in mind of a masculine version of the goddess Diana. By curious coincidence, excavations at the Romano-Celtic temple in Greenwich Park turned up what seemed to be part of a statue of Diana. It was an arm reaching back to extract an arrow from a quiver, a typical pose in which to portray Diana.

It has been necessary to discuss this matter at some length, because it enables us to get a grip upon the type of religion which was popular with the Celts in and around London. This may be summed up as having to do with horns, on either animals or humans. Camulus was a horned god, as was Pan, and the statue recovered from the well beneath Southwark Cathedral depicts a stag, which also of course has horns. At the temple in Greenwich Park, it seems likely that Diana was honoured, and her cult animal was also the stag. It is worth remembering too that another very popular deity for the Celts was Cernunnos, who was another human figure with horns sprouting from his head.

It is intriguing to find such signs of hunters and humans who share some characteristics with hunted beasts being venerated in the ancient area which would one day become London. Horns of course were symbolic of strength and power in Europe thousands of years ago. The largest and fiercest land animals all had horns or tusks, from the time of the Ice Age onwards; the mammoth, the woolly rhinoceros and then later the aurochs and the stag. These creatures may have been hunted and eaten, but they were also respected from their vigour and strength. This is of course why helmets were sometimes decorated with horns, to suggest that the person wearing it was as fearsome as a mad bull. Although such helmets are mentioned in Roman texts and shown in paintings, only one example has come down to us. The only such helmet ever found was dredged up from the Thames at Waterloo, hence its being known as the Waterloo Helmet. It may be seen in Illustration 12. The helmet is a beautiful piece of workmanship, being constructed of sheets of bronze. It is decorated with inlays of red glass. So striking is this object that it seems almost incredible that the owner should have lost it in the Thames without making the most strenuous efforts to recover it. The truth is, it was almost certainly not lost or misplaced, by deliberately thrown into the water.

The sacrifice of highly valued articles in the River Thames reached a crescendo in the years immediately before the Roman conquest. We are able to see this simply by looking at some of the things which have been recovered. It is this practice which most likely explains why no oppidum or even village was built in the area where London was established by the Romans. Before looking at what has been found and discussing the implications of such discoveries, a few words might not come amiss about the idea of sacrifice, which has fallen somewhat from favour in the country today.

For most people in London now, the act of giving to charity, or donating money to the collection taken during a church service, is very carefully calculated, and no more is sacrificed than is convenient. Although this is generally the case, there are still some churches where what is known as 'sacrificial giving' is undertaken. Suppose, for the sake of argument, that a church wishes to extend its building or even establish new premises somewhere. Under those circumstances, some members of the congregation may donate a very large sum of money, which they can only manage by foregoing something important. Perhaps they are planning to buy a new car or go on an expensive foreign holiday. Instead of doing so, the cost will be donated to the church as a sacrificial offering. This shows that the individual is prepared to give up something important for the sake of his or her faith. It need hardly be said that a man who gives the cost of a brand-new car in this way reaps a great deal of kudos among the other members of the church. Something similar was probably happening in and around the Thames thousands of years ago.

Illustration 13 shows a magnificent example of Celtic craftsmanship and art, in the style known as 'La Tène'. This is a ceremonial shield made from a single sheet of bronze and decorated with intricate, swirling patterns. It is also inlaid with red glass. This is far too fragile to have been used as a real shield in battle, such things usually being made of leather and wood. When new, this would have been shining like gold; imagine a brand-new copper coin and you will get the idea. The shield is in perfect condition and was dredged from the Thames at Battersea.

The idea has already been mentioned that items such as the Battersea Shield and the Waterloo Helmet were deliberately thrown into the Thames and that this practice had the effect of making the part of the Thames where London eventually was founded, a holy place. This might go some way towards explaining why nobody before the Roman came up with the idea of actually living near to that location. But what would motivate people to do such a thing? Why on earth would anybody commission a spectacular work of art and then just throw it away? To answer this question, we need to ask ourselves why this custom has persisted and why we still do pretty much the same today.

It is a fair assumption that most of those reading this book will, at some time or another, have thrown a coin into a body of water, in the vague hope that this will bring them good fortune. Sometimes, such offerings are made into fountains and wells and at others into rivers and lakes. This is of course where the idea of the 'wishing well' comes from, that by making an offering or sacrifice, some supernatural power might grant us aid. Of course, these days, our belief that this might actually happen are not altogether serious and yet still, we continue the custom.

When we deposit something in a river or well we are, even if we never think the matter through in a coherent fashion, hoping to strike a bargain with a chthonic deity. This means a god or goddess who wells beneath the earth in some underworld. Wells, holes in the ground, rivers, lakes and bogs may be thought of as portals to this hidden realm of the gods, which was also once thought to be the world of the dead. By making a gift of something valuable to those deities, it was believed possible to make a deal. In exchange for money or valuable goods, a god would undertake to interfere in the affairs of this world and help the supplicant achieve his purpose. The greater the favour which was solicited, the more significant must be the offering.

Many clues have been found in the Greater London area which shed light on what was going on here thousands of years ago, and also there is powerful evidence which enables us to understand the mental processes involved in the process of sacrifice. In an earlier chapter we looked at the Dagenham Idol and it was seen that this figure, dating back over 4,000 years to the very beginning of the Bronze Age, was probably an early form of the god Odin. It will be remembered that this figure was deliberately buried in a deep hole in the ground, accompanied by the antlers of a red deer. This indicates of course that the deposition was itself a gift to the gods who dwelt beneath the earth, but it reminds us too of something else which shed light upon the subject we are discussing.

The most important aspect of Odin or Woden's character, the thing which made him chief of the gods for the Saxons and Vikings, 3,000 years after the Dagenham Idol was buried in the marshlands by the Thames, was his wisdom. He did not content himself with casting a coin into a wishing well, but rather sacrificed one of his own eyes and left it in the well of Mímisbrunnr. It was this sacrifice which made him both the wisest of the gods and also marked him out as the only one-eyed god in the Indo-European pantheon.

It may seem that we have strayed somewhat from the question of what might have made the London area so significant before the coming of the Romans and why nobody before them had thought of building a large settlement here. In fact, we have now reached the crux of the matter. Not building homes or bases around what is now Westminster was a taboo which was based upon both the sacred and profane; both a matter of *realpolitik* and also a spiritual prohibition. That part of the Thames at Westminster and the City of London had a number of features which made it ideally suited as a focus for the ancient British people on more than one level.

Because the Thames was so very different 2,000 or 3,000 years ago, it is hard for us to visualize what the landscape might have looked like around the area which is now home to both the Houses of Parliament and the London Eye. For one thing, it would have been marshy, like the fens of East Anglia. The two rivers flowing into the Thames at this point, one from the east and the other from the west, would have produced a gravelly island in the middle of the Thames, one of the eyots which have earlier been mentioned. We looked in an earlier chapter at the likelihood that some kind of wooden construction led from the bank of the Thames to this spot, and it was likely that a platform stood here from which sacrifices were made. Although this little bridge had probably long since been swept away or rotted into nothing by the time of the Celtic culture which flourished shortly before the Roman invasion, the location itself would still have maintained its sanctity. Not only were weapons, tools, helmets and shields offered to the river in and around the ford at Westminster, there is also reason to suppose that a form of human sacrifice might also have been conducted here from time to time.

Most readers will probably be familiar with the so-called 'bog bodies' which have been recovered from bogs in Scandinavia, Germany, Ireland and England. Some of these date from the Iron Age and give every indication of having been ritually murdered for reasons at which we can only guess. What seems certain is that just as swords and shields were given to the gods who supposedly dwelt in watery places, so too were humans.

These are people who have been killed in unusual ways, for example by being garrotted or having their throats cut. What is especially notable is that some of them have been killed by combining two or three means of execution, that is to say that the victim was strangled and beaten while having his throat cut; surely a case of overkill!

Although no such bog bodies have been found in London, the number of skulls which seem to have been deposited both in the Thames and also its tributaries, such as the Walbrook, is quite remarkable. Various theories have been advanced for all the human heads which appear to have been thrown in rivers of central London during the Bronze Age and Iron Age. For one thing, it is suggested that these skulls were not deliberately places in rivers at all, but have rather been washed into streams such as the Walbrook from cemeteries, perhaps by erosion of the earth, combined with torrential rain. If this were so, then one might have expected to find ribcages and leg bones along with the skulls, but these are conspicuously lacking.

The Celts, both in Europe and Britain, subscribed to a cult which involved human heads. They regarded the head as the seat of the soul and therefore accorded it special reverence. Celtic warriors were often enthusiastic headhunters and some shrines have been discovered which had niches in them to place the severed heads of men slain in battle. Placing the heads of enemies in rivers had a symbolic significance which was probably associated with the idea that they thus became gifts to the gods. In 1907 a life-sized bronze head of the Roman emperor Claudius was found in the river Alde near Saxmundham in Suffolk. It had somehow been wrenched from a statue of Claudius which probably stood at Colchester, before the town was sacked by Boudicca in 61 AD. Hurling it into a river was perhaps something which naturally occurred to some Celtic rebel as being the proper way to dispose of an enemy's head.

We return to London and consider the matter of the huge numbers of skulls found buried in the ground or dredged up from rivers. The Walbrook is famous for being somewhere that skulls are often found. Although it was culverted over years ago, one can almost trace the course of this vanished river because of the skulls unearthed when digging foundations or excavating sewers along its course. In the late nineteenth century, what were described at the time as, 'immense numbers of skulls' were found during building works along the line of the Walbrook at Blomfield Street and Copthall Avenue in the City of London. It was guessed that these might be the decapitated heads of Roman soldiers, perhaps dating from the same period that the bronze head of Claudius was thrown into that river in Suffolk, that is to say the time of the Boudiccan revolt.

More recently, In the 1980s, a grisly discovery was made when digging the foundations for a bookshop at 54 London Wall. A total of thirty-nine skulls were dug up. During building work at Liverpool Street Station, another fifty skulls were found. All were dated to the centuries when the Romans lived in this part of London. The most noticeable feature about the skulls found along the Walbrook in the 1980s is that they most of them show signs of having been severed while the victims were alive.

Although very far from being a reliable chronicler of London's history, Geoffrey of Monmouth occasionally seemed to record what might be genuine folk memories or legends from the past. Writing in the twelfth century, he related that a detachment of Roman soldiers had been defeated in battle somewhere in central London and massacred beside a brook. Could this be an account of an actual event, handed down by word of mouth for a thousand years or so? It has been suggested that those detached skulls which are found in such profusion may be the decapitated heads of Romans who were captured by Boudicca and her army in around 60 AD, when Londinium fell and was destroyed by fire. In other words, those skulls are yet one more tangible sign of the practice of making sacrifices to the rivers of London, in this case, human sacrifices.

Life in the Thames Valley continued after Caesar left, much as it had done for centuries. There was perhaps a slightly more continental flavour than had been the case before the incursion by Roman forces. The people living there had been forcefully reminded that they were not quite as isolated as perhaps they had previously thought. There is evidence of more trade with Europe after Julius Caesar's expeditions. Writing some years after Caesar left, the Greek geographer Strabo said that;

Most of the island is flat and overgrown with forests, although many of its districts are hilly. It bears grain, cattle, gold, silver, and iron. These things, accordingly, are exported from the island, as also hides, and slaves, and dogs that are by nature suited to the purposes of the chase.

By which it will be seen that imports and exports were a two-way street. The Celts may well have been welcoming ships which sailed along the Thames from Europe, loaded with such exotic products as wine, but those same vessels returned to the Continent carrying gold, silver, iron and dogs. It was this trade which brought prosperity to late Iron Age Britain. And even if there was no actual settlement in that area which would become London, we can be fairly sure that it was there that the merchant ships landed their goods and took on fresh cargos, because the tide carried them up the Thames in this way to the heart of Britain.

Those years before the Roman conquest and the founding of a permanent settlement on the banks of the Thames, the small encampment which would one day become a mighty city, were good ones for Britain. The standard of living enjoyed by many people was higher than it had ever been before. The days though of independent tribes and chiefdoms in the land on either side of the Thames were fast drawing to a close. They came to an end with an event which struck the Britons like a thunderbolt, 97 years after Julius Caesar withdrew, following his second venture across the English Channel.

Chapter 8

The Roman Conquest

After Julius Caesar left Britain in 54 BC, it was to be almost a century before the Romans took any further interest in the British Isles. Over the course of that time, there was increasing contact between Britain and mainland Europe by way of trading. Graves have been found from this period which contain amphorae of wine, placed there for the dead to enjoy in the afterlife. These can only have been imported from the Continent. There are other indications too that Celtic Britain, or at least members of the elite, had begun to copy the way of life and customs which were spreading through the Romanised parts of Europe. During this time the Catuvellauni continued to become more powerful in East Anglia and that part of South East Britain which lay north of the Thames. The most important of the oppida at this time was Camulodunon, which was to become the city of Camulodunum during the Roman occupation, and is now known as Colchester.

In 41 AD, an event took place almost 1,500km from the Thames Valley, which was to result in the foundation of a city on the banks of the Thames; a region in which nobody had ever chosen to live in settlements larger than a single farm. This was the assassination in Rome of the Emperor Caligula. Caligula's reign had been marked by cruelty and degeneracy, and the excesses of the emperor had become so grotesque that the army decided to depose him. After his murder, the army also killed his wife and child. It must have looked as though the intention was perhaps to wipe out the imperial family and one can hardly blame Claudius, the middle-aged nephew of the emperor, for assuming that he might also fall victim to those who had overthrown his uncle and slaughtered some members of his family. In the event though, when soldiers found Claudius, who was hiding behind a curtain in terror of his life, it was decided that he might make a suitable emperor and so with the backing of the army, he was announced as ruler of the Roman Empire.

It is altogether possible that proclaiming Claudius as emperor was seen as a shrewd tactical move on the part of those who had overthrown Caligula. The new emperor was a quiet, studious man who had written a number of academic works on history and might perhaps have seemed like somebody who would rule in name only and allow the army to do pretty well as they pleased. If this is how the minds of senior officers had been working when they chose Claudius for the position, then they were to find that they had been greatly mistaken. It was a mistake which was to have momentous consequences for Britain just two years later and to lead to the foundation of London.

Since Julius Caesar had left the country in 54 BC, the tribe of the Catuvellauni had gone from strength to strength and they were not favourably disposed towards Rome. Those organizing attacks on the Roman army in Gaul knew that they had only to slip across the English Channel and they would be able to escape the Romans and rest and recuperate, before returning to mainland Europe to cause more trouble. This was annoying to the Romans, and Caligula had been planning a punitive expedition shortly before he was assassinated. For Claudius, Britain provided a perfect way of achieving two aims at once. In the first place, invading and occupying Britain would show that he was a powerful leader and no mere puppet of the army. He would achieve what the famous Julius Caesar had failed to do. The second reason for the expedition was pragmatic and a consequence of his nephew's murder. Claudius could see clearly that it was the army who were likely to pose a threat to his life as the years passed, if his rule was displeasing to them. Conquering Britain would necessitate a large army of occupation to maintain the new province as part of the empire. This meant that tens of thousands of soldiers, along with many senior officers, would be permanently exiled, a good long way from Rome. That portion of the army at least would not have the leisure to plot against Claudius or try to devise ways of overthrowing him.

In 43 AD, 97 years after Roman troops left Britain, a huge army landed on the south coast, consisting of around 40,000 men. The Romans were aware that the main population centre at which they needed to aim was Camulodunon, in what is now Essex. To reach it, the troops would of course be obliged to cross the Thames and it was in this way that the destiny of London began.

The geography of Britain dictated two things, when once the Romans had been ordered to launch an attack on the oppidum of Camulodunon. The first was that to get an army to Britain from the European mainland in the swiftest and safest way, it would be necessary to land it on the south coast, in either Sussex or Kent. Secondly, of course, before the oppidum could be reached, the Thames would need to be crossed. Unless a bridge was to be built, then this would mean fording the river at the first convenient point upstream from the Thames estuary, which meant the area which we now know as Westminster. It will be remembered that what came to be known as Watling Street, the Roman road which led from Kent to London, existed before the Roman conquest and led directly to the ford. All that the invaders would have needed to do was to head north from their landing place and they would then strike the track leading west to the ford.

What was to be found in the London area at this time? We cannot say for certain, although there is some evidence. We know that fields were being ploughed in Bermondsey, which suggests that there were probably a few farms on the south side of the river in that area. We know too that there were collections of barrows standing on the brow of hills as one walked along what would one day be Watling Street. It would probably have been a fairly bleak landscape. It is possible that there was some kind of cult centre around what is now Vauxhall and Westminster, but this is speculation and deduction, based upon the wooden posts which we have seen jutting up from the riverbed there. There were probably temples too, in Southwark and Greenwich. Certainly, there was no large settlement of any kind.

The Thames served as a natural border between the Catuvellauni and Trinovantes in the north, the territory which is now Essex, Suffolk, Hertfordshire and so on, and the Atrebates and Canti, who had their lands south of the river. So powerful had the Catuvellauni become, that it is entirely possible that the Atrebates felt menaced by them and could foresee a time that they would fall under their domination.

For this reason, it is not improbable that the advancing Roman army would have received help in finding the ford, as well as information about the disposition of the forces on the opposing bank at the ford. Julius Caesar was given such help in locating the oppidum of the Catuvellauni during his second expedition to Britain.

The army of the Catuvellauni defended the ford and tried to prevent the Roman forces from crossing, but this was achieved after some fierce fighting. It was then necessary to secure the north bank of the river, so that a battle would not need to be fought every time a detachment of men tried to cross the Thames. In this way, the ford at Westminster was, from the very beginning of the enterprise, of great military significance. There was a problem though, which was that the area around the ford was marshy and wet. This part of the north bank of the Thames was known in medieval times as Thorney Island, because the two branches of the Tyburn which entered the Thames here did indeed make it an island. It was, well into the Middle Ages, known too as Bulinga Fen. A fen it was, swampy and unhealthy. It was a most unsuitable place for a permanent camp and so plans were soon laid for a better arrangement for crossing the river, other than wading across the Thames and then finding oneself in a waterlogged fen.

Obviously, a ferry or bridge would be far more convenient than a ford and in this way a crossing might be effected which was secure and guarded at both ends. We have seen that along the Thames were various gravel islands and there were also low gravel hills which were well drained and consequently dry. These made ideal places to establish marching camps; a type of temporary fort. The first of these was set up on the tallest hill in central London, upon which today stands the church of St Peter's Cornhill. This hill is not particularly high – the crest is less than 60ft above sea level – but it was the best to be found. A small river which we now call the Walbrook ran along one side of the hill and the Thames was to the south. Once another camp had been built on a gravel island across the river in Southwark, the Roman army had, unwittingly, laid the foundations for the mighty city which would one day stand here.

It is here that the first bridge across the Thames was built, and it would have connected the Roman camp with some of the marshy islands which made up Southwark at that time. We know that farming was being practised on some of the islands and that there were at least two barrows, which were found a few years ago in that area. Almost certainly though, nobody was actually living in Southwark, any more than they were in what is now the City of London and so the Romans had what amounted to a blank slate, to impose their own ideas of how a city should be developed here.

We have reached the end of our account of prehistoric London, because from this point onwards we have written mentions of what happened in Britain. This is when the history of London actually began, and we can even consult inscriptions which tell us that the name London was being used for this part of Britain. The history of London starts with the founding of a settlement in which lived men and women who were literate. We have a wealth of evidence for what was happening in this part of Britain and we no longer have to rely upon scanty remains such as piles of earth on hilltops or vague traces of ploughed land by the riverside.

Endword

The fact that there are no written accounts of those living in or visiting prehistoric London has not hindered archaeologists in building up an accurate picture of what this part of Britain was like in the distant past. Indeed, as in court cases, circumstantial evidence is often more accurate, reliable and trustworthy than that of witnesses. This is all the more so when examining history, because there is no such thing as neutral and unbiased history. Everybody writing or speaking about a particular place during a specific time has his or her own perspective and background, and these work subconsciously to distort and slant any narrative, no matter how objective the author hopes it to be. This is not the case with fossils and bones, although even then the interpretation of such things can of course be flawed.

Despite these reservations, it has proved possible to put together a coherent and reasonably accurate story of the London area over the last 150 million years or so. Doubtless some details are lacking and others will be proved incorrect by later research, but the broad picture is unlikely to change dramatically in coming years. What is fascinating is that the events of the prehistoric past are every bit as dramatic and noteworthy as those of later times. We all know about the Norman invasion in 1066 and the Spanish Armada, but the invasion of Britain by Neolithic farmers or the coming of the

Yamnaya from the east are of no less interest. Indeed, they are of far more significant than the recorded history of this country, because they entailed far greater changes, both in lifestyle and population.

William the Conqueror's invasion of England and seizure of the throne in 1066 is an event known to us all, and seen as pivotal in the history of Britain. Yet there were at the time of the invasion almost two million people living in Britain and no more than 10,000 Normans came over to the country in the wake of William's victory. In other words, the 'invasion' consisted of the arrival of a new population consisting of just 0.5 per cent of the number of people already living in Britain. When we compare this with the wholesale replacement of the existing population which took place first during the Neolithic and then later when the Bronze Age began, it is easy to see that these events were of stupendous significance compared with what happened in 1066. Just because we have no Bayeux Tapestry to record the coming of the Yamnaya to Britain, does not mean that it was not noteworthy.

It is probably fair to say that an understanding of prehistoric London will equip us with an understanding of the changes which the country as a whole has undergone over the millennia. The clues about life in the Thames Valley over the millennia is a microcosm of life in Britain as a whole. The Greater London area is like a time capsule, with the remains of every element of British prehistory preserved *in situ* and able to be examined for the cost of a journey by bus or Tube train. Studying the sites found in London will enable anybody to trace the story of this country from the time of the dinosaurs up to the beginning of recorded history.

Appendix: Prehistoric Sites which can be Visited in London

Asurprising number of sites in London which date from before the Roman invasion in 43 AD are on open display and may be visited at any time. These are listed below in chronological order, starting with the seabed from the Eocene Era, 55 million years ago.

Abbey Wood Fossil Bed
Lesnes Abbey Woods Local Nature Reserve
London SE2 0AX
The nearest railway station to this site is Abbey Wood, and the nature reserve and woods lie about a kilometre South East of the station. The best place to begin is the ruins of Lesnes Abbey, which was established here roughly 900 years ago, before being destroyed during the Reformation. There are maps of the wood on public noticeboards here, which show clearly how to reach the fossil bed. This is to be found on a low plateau, surrounded by trees. It may be seen in Illustration 4.

Although a rough wooden fence encircles the sandy area of the fossil bed, access is open and free. This is simply the ancient seabed which once lay beneath the tropical lagoon which many millions of years ago made up the area we now know as London. All that is necessary to uncover for yourself the evidence of this astonishing fact is to dig in the sand. For this purpose, it is wise to bring a trowel and also an ordinary sieve, so that the sand may be sifted through for the marine fossils which are to be found here in great abundance. Illustration 5 gives some idea of what is likely to be found.

There are one or two rules when visiting the fossil bed, but these are no more than common sense and not at all onerous. For instance, you are requested to fill in any holes which you have left, on leaving the site. Holes deeper than 2ft are not allowed and nor is removing more than half a kilogram of fossils. Apart from this though, anybody is welcome to visit this fragment of the ancient past and spend an afternoon in the pursuit of practical palaeontology.

Mesolithic Structure in the Thames
Headquarters of the Secret Intelligence Service
85 Albert Embankment, London SE1 7TP

The easiest way of finding the remains of the earliest human activity in London is to head for the MI6 building in Vauxhall and then make your way down to the Thames foreshore, directly beneath the building. The wooden posts are only visible at the very lowest tide and anybody wishing to see them will have to make their visit during what is known as a 'spring tide'. This has no bearing upon the season, but is a particularly low tide which occurs twice a month. Even when they are visible, the wooden posts which can be glimpsed are not particularly exciting or memorable, but are without doubt the oldest structure in London. Carbon-dating tells us that they were erected here around 6,500 years ago.

Neolithic Long Barrow
Richmond Park
Richmond, TW10 5HS

Richmond Park is the only place in Greater London where a Bronze Age round barrow may be compared with a long barrow from the Neolithic. The nearest station to Richmond Park is Richmond, which is both a British Rail and London Underground station. From the station, it is a fairly easy walk up Richmond Hill to the park itself. On entering the park, it is necessary to veer to the right, walking along Queen's Road, and then following signs which indicate the way to King Henry's Mound. It is about 700 yards from the gate by which you entered. This is a round barrow from the Bronze Age and is worth visiting for the spectacular view across London which may be obtained at the top. Looking west, one can see Windsor Castle and in the opposite direction, St Paul's Cathedral. Which means of course, that this barrow would have been visible on a clear day from a distance of 10 miles to the east or west.

On leaving King Henry's Mound, one must follow the footpath which runs parallel to Queen's Road. Continue along it, passing the information centre and Pembroke Lodge on the right. After a quarter of a mile or so, the path turns sharply to the left, but a footpath leads straight ahead to the Long Barrow. Access is partly blocked by branches woven around posts to knee height. This is to prevent erosion by cyclists. It is at once obvious that this barrow is indeed long, compared with the circular King Henry's Mound. Although it is now more oval than rectangular, it is likely that this is due to the effects of

5,000 years of wind and rain and that at one time it was more clearly defined. Like the round barrow at which we have just looked, this too would have been visible for many miles, being perched on the very edge of a steep slope. In the winter, when the trees are bare, it is possible to look south from here, across the Thames, and see the Surrey Hills as far as Box Hill.

Lodge Road Neolithic Track
Epping Forest
Epping Road, Epping Forest, CM16 5HW
Walking along the footpath, which is now Lodge Road, near Epping, is a strange experience. It is possible to see exactly how and why the track was originally constructed and what the consequences have been over the 4,000 years since it was laid down. There is a car park at the beginning of Lodge Road. Leaving this and starting to walk along the track, you can see at once the lie of the land and understand why some people in the late Neolithic or early Bronze Age went to the trouble of building the path. To the north, that is to your right as you walk along Lodge Road from the car park, are many springs. They used to flow south and the run over the edge of the low plateau. This meant that all the land here was marshy and waterlogged throughout the whole year. Building the track which is now Lodge Road had the effect of damming those streams and preventing them from flowing down to the lower ground. This meant that the water accumulated to the north of the path and became a bog, rather than merely an area of sodden marsh. There are signs warning of the danger posed by the deep bog, an unusual sight so close to London.

Winn's Common Tumulus
Winn Common Road, London SE18 2AA

The nearest station to Winn's Common is the British Rail one of Plumstead. Heading east along Plumstead High Street, on leaving the station, will bring you after a kilometre or so to a turning on your right called Riverdale Road. This leads to the common, which is a bleak expanse of grass. The tumulus lies immediately in front of you as you arrive at the common after walking down Riverdale Road.

It has to be said that the barrow on Winn's Common, also known as Plumstead Common, is not all that impressive, as may be seen from Illustration 2. It is little more than a circular bump on the grass, about 20 yards across and no more than a yard high. It is only because the local authority does not mow the barrow, as they do the surrounding common, that it is even possible to identify it. There were at one time half a dozen similar barrows here, but the others have long since been flattened. Not far away is another single round barrow which, like this one, is the only survivor or a group which have been erased. This is the so-called Shrewsbury Barrow.

The Shrewsbury Barrow
Junction of Brinklow Crescent and Plum Lane, London SE18 3BP

If you wish to reach Shrewsbury Barrow after visiting the tumulus on Winn's Common, then it is necessary to walk west, along the southern edge of Plumstead Common, which lies adjacent to Winn's Common. Plumstead Common Road delineates this side of Plumstead Common, which will be on your right as you walk along. Eventually, a turning on the left called Plum Lane will be seen and this leads up to the slopes of Shooters Hill. The crest of Shooters Hill is one of the highest points in Greater London.

Shrewsbury Barrow may be found on the right, as you walk up the hill. It is at the junctions with Brinklow Crescent. There were, until the 1930s, six barrows in this area, but the others were dug up and built over when the houses were built here. Across the road is a piece of woodland and next to it a park. It was here that the earliest evidence for the extraction and forging of iron has been found in London, possibly the whole of Britain.

Iron railings surround the barrow and there is an interpretation panel, which explains what is seen. Without this information, it is unlikely that anybody would give a second look at this grassy hillock. It is 25 yards across and about a yard and a half high. The buildings here obscure the view now, but when the hillside was in its natural state, this barrow and the others would have been visible for miles. The barrow may be seen in Illustration 15.

Greenwich Barrow Cemetery
Greenwich Park
London SE10 8QY

Greenwich Park contains two intriguing relics of the past, but the history of both is uncertain and relies upon speculation. The first of these features is a field of over thirty barrows, which lies at the top of a steep hill and offers a wonderful view of the towers of Docklands. This strange landscape is to be found just inside the Croom Hill entrance to the park.

The nearest station to Greenwich Park is the Docklands Light Railway Station for the Cutty Sark. All that is needed is to walk up Croom Hill from there and to turn left into the park at the top of the hill. The cemetery may be seen in Illustration 11.

That the area of grassland is covered in ancient burial mounds is certain. What is less sure is how old these barrows are. Some are without doubt Saxon, the evidence being provided when a few were opened. It is however conjectured that the Saxons adopted this site for their own burials because there were already barrows here, which dated back to the Bronze Age. This is a plausible hypothesis, because of course the reuse of sites originally belonging to an earlier culture was common in Britain.

Most of the barrows at Greenwich are small. Some are barely more than bumps or dimples in the grass and even the larger ones might are barely noticeable, unless you happen to be looking for them. It is the position of this barrow field, right at the top of a hill, with a view to the Thames below, which makes it an ideal spot for men in the Bronze Age to have chosen. It is, in this sense, very similar to the position of the barrows which were once to be found on the side of Shooters Hill.

Speculation about these barrows being a case of a Bronze Age site appropriated by later occupiers of the land is lent support by the fact that they are just half a kilometre from the remains of a Roman-Celtic temple. Signposts throughout the park indicate the way to this site. Such temples were frequently established on earlier places of worship and so the close proximity of both the temple and the barrow field does suggest that there was something special about this location. The earthworks of the temple may be seen in Illustration 16.

Boadicea's Grave
Parliament Hill Fields
London NW5 1QR

There is no reason whatsoever to think that this barrow has any connection, however tenuous, with the Iceni queen, but it is certainly the finest example of a Bronze Age barrow to be found in London and of an unusual type into the bargain. It may be seen in Illustration 14. The easiest way of finding this barrow is to go to the top of Parliament Hill, alongside Hampstead Heath.

Boadicea's Grave is a type of burial mound known as a bell barrow, because that is what such things look like in cross section. They are the rarest kind of barrow, and most are to be found in Wiltshire and Dorset, rather than south-east England. Bell barrows are constructed in the following fashion. First, a 'quarry ditch' is dug, and then the spoil heaped up into the centre of the circular platform so formed. This makes bell barrows more visually striking than other round barrows. This one was opened in the nineteenth century, but all that was found was charred remains. Because of the lack of a body, a story began to circulate that rather than a burial mound, this might rather have been a rubbish dump dating from only a century or so ago. Why anybody should have carted their rubbish all the way up this hill to bury it is an interesting point!

Anybody visiting Boadicea's Grave today will notice at once that it is on the edge of a steep escarpment and that the view extends for some miles to the north.

Loughton Camp and Amesbury Banks

The best way of reaching these two sites is to go to the small Essex town of Loughton, which lies on the Central Line of the

London Underground. From there, they may be reached on foot. The two Iron Age hill forts which lie in Epping Forest are not very impressive to look at today, consisting of little more than vague undulations, which indicate where the banks and ditches of the fortifications once were. Unless you had been told what you were looking at, it would be easy to miss these remains entirely.

Both Loughton Camp and Amesbury Banks date from roughly the same period, which is to say a few centuries before the Roman invasion in 43 AD. To find them, it is necessary to explore the forest on foot, for there are no carparks nearby. One is to be found in the forest near to the town of Loughton and the other is positioned midway between Loughton and the town of Epping. Neither of these two sites is large. They are both roughly 10 acres in area, which is roughly the equivalent of six football pitches. This makes it unlikely that they were villages, more probable is that they were places of refuge when there were skirmishes between neighbouring tribes.

Loughton Camp is positioned on a very high point in Epping Forest, which would have made it an ideal lookout post, while Amesbury Banks is on level ground. It is possible that the purpose of Amesbury Banks was connected in some way with Lodge Road, the late Neolithic track which lies about 500 yards to the west and predates the hill fort by 2,000 years or so. It is not inconceivable that this track was of great importance during the Iron Age and Amesbury Banks served as a customs post or border control or something of the kind.

So negligible are the remains at both of these sites, that it was only in the nineteenth century that it was realized that these were hill forts. Without modern archaeological excavations, it is often impossible to distinguish ancient remains from more modern constructions. At High Beech, for instance, also in Epping Forest, it was for a long time maintained that the little hillocks known as the pillow mounds, were in fact prehistoric barrows. We know now that they are actually the remains of rabbit warrens set up only a century or two ago, to provide a handy supply of meat.

Charlton Camp

This Iron Age hill fort, which was occupied about 300 BC, is close to the oppidum which was discovered at Woolwich. Both are within walking distance of the Woolwich Arsenal railway station. Turning right after leaving that station and then taking the next left turn, you will find yourself walking north along Beresford Street. The Thames is on the right-hand side, behind a new building development. It was in this area, between Beresford Street and the river, that the closest oppidum to central London was found in 1986, following the demolition of the Woolwich power station. It remained a secret for many years, because archaeologists were afraid that treasure hunters would descend upon the site and begin unauthorized digs there.

There is nothing to see of the oppidum today, but since it was founded shortly after the hill fort at which we are going to look was abandoned, there may perhaps be a connection between the two places. If we continue walking along Beresford Street, it becomes Church Street once we pass the terminal of the Woolwich Ferry. This will lead in due course to a turning on the left called Prospect Vale and then to a road on the right called Maryon Park Road. This takes us to the park where the hill fort is to be found.

The remaining part of Charlton Camp is known today as Cox's Mount and it may be found in the northernmost part of Maryon Park. Steps lead to the small plateau at the top, which was once much larger. So much quarrying for sand and gravel has taken place here over the years, that much of the hill fort has been simply dug up and carried off. With the trend during the later years of the Iron Age to stop using hill forts like this and instead to make settlements on lower land, surrounded by ditches and banks, it may be that those who lived here built the oppidum at Woolwich.

Greenwich Temple
Greenwich Park
Blackheath Avenue
Greenwich
London
SE10 8XJ

It is not certain that this site was indeed a prehistoric one, but the balance of probabilities is that it was. This was without doubt the location of a Roman temple and many Romano-Celtic temples were built on pre-existing British places of worship or pilgrimage. All that may be seen today of the temple is some retaining banks which would have formed the platform on which the temple building itself was erected. There are signs in Greenwich Park which point the way to the temple and there is too an informative sign there, which describes what has been found here.

The original track which the Romans turned into Watling Street passed near this spot, which makes it all the more likely that it was a place of some significance for those who lived in this part of Britain before the Roman conquest. Traces of Watling Street were uncovered during excavations a few years ago here for a television programme. Nearby, at the top of a hill next to the Royal Observatory, is a field of circular burial mounds. It is certain that some of these were made by the Saxons, but there is a strong suspicion that before they arrived here, there was already a cemetery here, which was established during the Bronze Age. The close proximity of both the nearby track which was to become Watling Street, and also other barrows in nearby areas, lends credence to the idea.

Wimbledon Common Hill Fort
Windmill Car Park
Windmill Road
London
SW19 5NQ
It takes some dedication to track down and examine the remains of the hill fort on Wimbledon Common. Unless one knew beforehand just what it is that one was looking at, it is unlikely in the extreme that it would be possible to guess what these bumps in the ground signify.

Valence House Museum
Becontree Avenue
Dagenham
RM8 3HT
The Dagenham Idol, the earliest representation of a human figure in England, may be found in this museum. It was found

nearby in the 1920s and has been carbon-dated to around 2250 BC. This strange figure sheds light on the religious beliefs which were current at the time that it was buried in marshland. The museum also contains flints and bronze weapons found in the district.

The British Museum
Great Russell Street
London WC1B 3DG

Most of the prehistoric artifacts mentioned in this book as having been found in London, may be seen in this museum. These include things such as the Battersea Shield, the Waterloo Helmet and many other weapons and tools which were deposited in the Thames as votive offerings.

Bibliography

Ackroyd, Peter (2011), *London Under*, London, Chatto & Windus.

Attenborough, David (1987), *The First Eden*, London, William Collins.

Brothwell, Don (1986), *The Bog Man and the Archaeology of People*, London, British Museum Publications.

Cavalli-Sforza, Luigi (2000), *Genes, Peoples and Languages*, London, Penguin Press.

Clayton, Antony (2000), *Subterranean City: Beneath the Streets of London*, London, Historical Publications

Clout, Hugh (ed.), *The Times London History Atlas*, London, Times Books.

Cunliffe, Barry (2003), *The Celts: A Very Short Introduction*, Oxford, Oxford University Press

Cunliffe, Barry (ed.) (1994), *The Oxford Illustrated Prehistory of Europe*, Oxford, Oxford University Press.

Curtis, Sue (2004), *Ilford: A History*, Chichester, Philimore.

Dinnis, Rob & Stringer, Chris (2014), *Britain – One Million Years of the Human Story*, London, The Natural History Museum.

Evans, Brian (1989), *Bygone Ilford*, Chichester, Philimore.

Farndon, John (1994), *Dictionary of the Earth*, London, Dorling Kindersley.

Fortey, Richard (1993), *The Hidden Landscape*, London, Johnathon Cape.

Green, Miranda J. (1983), *The Gods of Roman Britain*, Princes Risborough, Shire Publications.

Jones, Steve (1996), *In the Blood*, London, HarperCollins.

Manley, Johns (2002), *AD 43: The Roman Invasion of Britain*, Stroud, Tempus Publishing.

Merriman, Nick (1990), *Prehistoric London*, London, HMSO.

Moffat, Alastair (2017), *Britain – A Genetic Journey*, Edinburgh, Berlinn.

Oppenheimer, Stephen, (2006), *The Origins of the British*, London, Constable & Robinson.

Papagianni, Dimitra & Morse, Michael A. (2013), *The Neanderthals Rediscovered*, London, Thames & Hudson.

Richards, Julian (1999), *Meet the Ancestors*, London, BBC Worldwide.

Roberts, Alice (2021), *Ancestors: The Prehistory of Britain in Seven Burials*, London, Simon & Schuster UK.

Roberts, Nyda (1994), *The Bronze Age: A Time of Change*, Telford, Signal House Publications.

Scarre, Chris (1998), *Exploring Prehistoric Europe*, Oxford, Oxford University Press.

Shuckburgh, Julian (1998), *London Revealed*, Oxford, Oxford University Press.

Trench, Richard & Hillman, Ellis (1985), *London Under London: A Subterranean Guide*, London, John Murray

Wacher, John (1979), *The Coming of Rome*, London, Routledge & Kegan Paul.

Webb, Simon (2011), *Unearthing London*, Stroud, The History Press.

Williams, Brenda (2006), *Ancient Britain*, Andover, Jerrold Publishing.

Woodward, Ann (1992), *Shrines and Sacrifice*, London, B.T. Batsford.

Index